THE SAUCY TALES UNCLE ALBERT
AND HIS FRIENDS

A Collection of Humorous Tales of
Uncle Albert and His Friends

Written and illustrated by Anthony Todd
Published by Christmas Cottage Publications

Designed by Jane Thomas
& Piers Plummer

Copyright © Anthony Todd 2013
All rights reserved

uncle-albert@tony-todd.co.uk

Christmas Cottage Publications
65, New Road, Chilworth,
Guildford, Surrey, GU4 8LU

With Special Thanks to:

Iris
Jane
Piers
Trysh
Chris
Poppy
Daisy

and all who gave encouragement
in the publishing of this book.

UNCLE ALBERT STORIES

Uncle Albert, the Romantic 5
The Attempted Bribery of Miss Crisp 7
Uncle Albert Takes Brenda to the Posh Tea Shop 9
Up the City! 11
Honeysuckle Rose and a Soggy Sponge 13
Ice Cream for Three 15
The Office 17
Visit to the Mango-Calypso Bar 19
Uncle Albert's Birthday Lunch
    Making a Day of It 21
    Fluttering Eyelashes and Thrusting Bosoms 23
    Posh Champagne and Sunglasses 25
    Spike and Dusty Hoover Up 27
    Let's See Your Thong, Troy 29
    The Goose and the Traffic Cone 32
    Squeak, Squeak, Squeak 35
    Absolute Nectar 37
No Crab for Me 39
In the Sack with Amanda 41
I Hate Gulls 43
A Night Out at the Plaza Ballroom 45
In The Butchers Arms 47
Up, Up and Away 49
Best Leeks in Show 51
Uncle Albert takes Brenda out 53
The 'Borrowed' Scooter 55
Flaming June 57
Did Anyone see the Blazing Firecrest? 59
The Lucky Rabbit 61

The Village Characters

DOTTY A very sporty widow indeed who loves flowers and cooking. She has won medals for skating.

BRENDA She loves the sea and has a huge collection of Ray-Burn sunglasses. She snores loudly, doesn't like crabs but is partial to drinking exotic cocktails. She can also change car tyres in record time.

AMANDA Loves dancing and often takes Uncle Albert to the Plaza. She won the sack race at last year's fete.

SPIKE AND DUSTY Uncle Albert's two dogs. They are always hungry – they follow Billy Boothright around the village because he smells of meat pies. Dusty tends to wee uncontrollably when he sees Miss Crisp. Spike once had a love affair with a stuffed rabbit.

DOGEND DEREK Pigeon owner, goes to bed with his hat on, rolls his own cigarettes and has an orange coloured upper lip.

MISS CRISP The dog-show judge, she is very prim and proper but has a very soft spot for Micky Finn. the fish man.

DANCING DAVE Fine wine and champagne producer of distinction. He keeps ferrets and once had a reputation for his expert dancing. His knees have given up on him so now so he just drinks.

BILLY BOOTHRIGHT He loves his food, especially his mum's food in very large quantities. He is not especially successful with the opposite sex, but his mum loves him.

RUPERT He works in the off-licence and is chairman of the Bird Spotting Club, also captain of the Bowls Club. He was the manager of Stiff & Partners, the undertakers, owns a large field and has a fondness for geese.

QUICKSTEP CHRIS Plays the trombone for a dance quartet and says he is an expert on vintage champagne.

TROY The assistant at the Regal coffee bar. Since working there coffee sales have soared through the roof.

GEORGE An allotment holder who has won prizes for his cider which he usually drinks before he can bottle it.

PHIL Another allotment holder who also makes cider. Another quick guzzler.

MICKY FINN He runs a wet fish shop and is a pigeon fancier. He loves Miss Crisp unconditionally and has a particular fascination for her thrusting bosom.

MONTY Friend of Arthur Crown, an expert on double digging and growing radishes.

OLD JONNIE ROTTEN Looks much older than he is due to heavy smoking when he was a teenager. Knowledgeable about pigeons, ferrets, and Tesco shares. Needs a bit of dental work done.

JULIAN Troy's partner, envy of the majority of the females in the village.

ARTHUR CROWN Grows rhubarb and is best friend of Monty. Has a thing about wheelbarrows.

Uncle Albert

THE SAUCY TALES OF UNCLE ALBERT AND HIS FRIENDS

Uncle Albert is getting on a bit but still feels young at heart with an urge to enjoy his second childhood.

He has several lady friends, Dotty, Brenda and Amanda, who all think he is charming on a good day, but without doubt grumpy on a bad day! They sometimes go with him to the cinema or the coast and sometimes, if there is a dance on, they get him to go to the Plaza Ballroom for a slow romantic waltz. They like to keep an eye on him.

Very often, to escape for some peace and quiet, he will visit his allotment which boasts a shed almost as old as himself. He grows dahlias for Dotty, a very sporty widow indeed, who lives at number 33, Corporation Avenue, and who cooks a Sunday Roast that just melts in your mouth. A fair exchange, he always thinks, a bunch of flowers for a Sunday dinner! Uncle Albert also grows tomatoes and has become well known for his "Golden Burst" tomatoes, which he grows with the aid of a secret formula; a most evil smelling, sludge like liquid, that "makes them tommies the sweetest you'll ever taste".

Uncle Albert has two dogs that idolise him and slurpingly help to clear his plate at mealtimes. They also keep his war wounds warm during the winter evenings, something he will never talk about, unless, of course, you're asking.

He is good at crosswords, likes dog racing, and swears by Tesco's red wine. All in all, he likes his quiet life; that is until the urge to do something new and exciting takes over. Then Uncle Albert can become a completely different animal!

Uncle Albert, the Romantic

Uncle Albert is a newcomer to ice skating, but since Dotty introduced him to it last year, he has progressed so well he is considering buying his own skates and a season ticket to the local rink.

But he has a problem, which he wants to keep to himself; he can only skate in a clockwise direction. So if Dotty wants him to go the other way, they usually end up flat on the ice with Uncle Albert blaming her for tripping him up!

However, he has found that if he continually skates in a clockwise direction he can cut a pretty good impression of a heart shape in the ice. Because of this, Dotty thinks he is very romantic, and, in spite of all the falls and bruises, thinks she may have found his tender side.

Uncle Albert sometimes wonders if Dotty is all there and tells her not to be so silly.

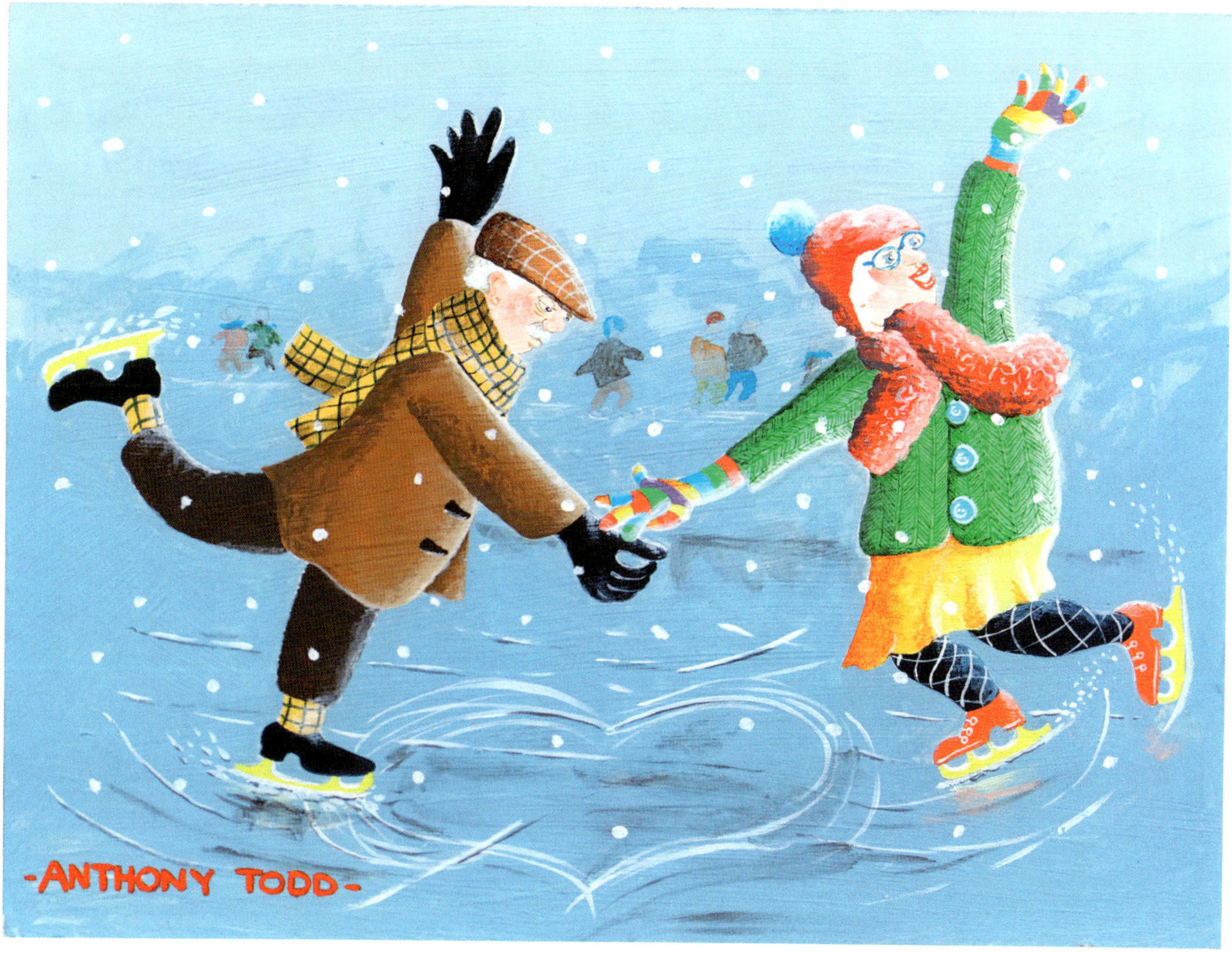
-ANTHONY TODD-

The Attempted Bribery of Miss Crisp

Dusty is Uncle Albert's pooch and loves taking part in dog shows. Dusty comes from great stock, his mother, Lily, won the cup for "The Dog Most Like his Owner" for seven years on the trot. But she failed to win the cup on the eighth year when her owner decided to have a facelift, to correct a rather jowly look, and ended up looking nothing like Lily!

This year Uncle Albert thought the judge, Miss Crisp, was biased after Dusty peed over her new, expensive Hush Puppies. Dusty had no idea they were new or expensive. Uncle Albert tried to calm troubled waters by asking if she would be a sport and accept a bottle of Dancing Dave's Turnip and Carrot Sparkling Champagne and then perhaps they could forget the whole unfortunate matter.

Miss Crisp has since banned them both from entering all dog shows for life, for attempted bribery.

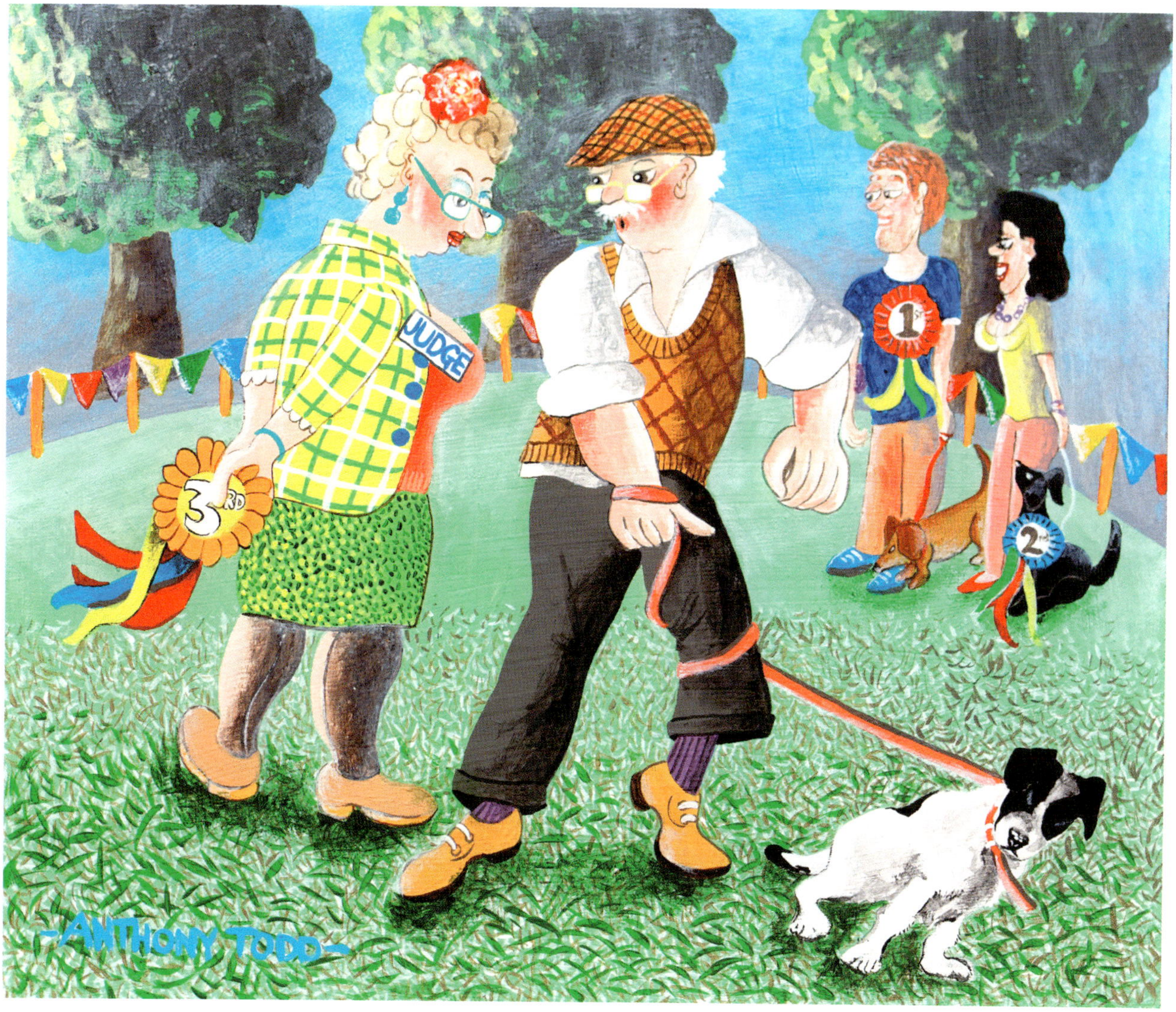
JUDGE
3RD
1ST
2ND
-ANTHONY TODD-

Uncle Albert takes Brenda to The Posh Tea Shop

Brenda thinks Uncle Albert is so clever because he never uses a Sat-Nav when he is cruising along in his Austin Seven. In fact he hasn't got a Sat-Nav, but he has been known to get lost.

Sometime ago he went up the Motorway the wrong way and it cost him his week's pension to pay for the petrol to get back home again. Dotty had to come round and treat him for shock.

Today though, he is only going a few miles down the road to The Posh Tea Shop. He makes out he can't resist the cream and jam scones they serve. But really he is trying to impress Brenda by acting as if he is quite used to going to posh tea shops. He hates scones, they make him feel queasy. He would much rather have a nice sausage roll with lashings of tomato ketchup, but they don't do those in The Posh Tea Shop. Uncle Albert cuts his scone and offers half to Brenda. "What a gentleman!" she says, drenching her portion in thick cream and jam. She devours it in seconds, smacking her highly glossed lips loudly.

Uncle Albert sips his tea in his gentlemanly fashion, and dreams of the deep fried haddock and chips with mushy peas and bread and butter he will be having for dinner.

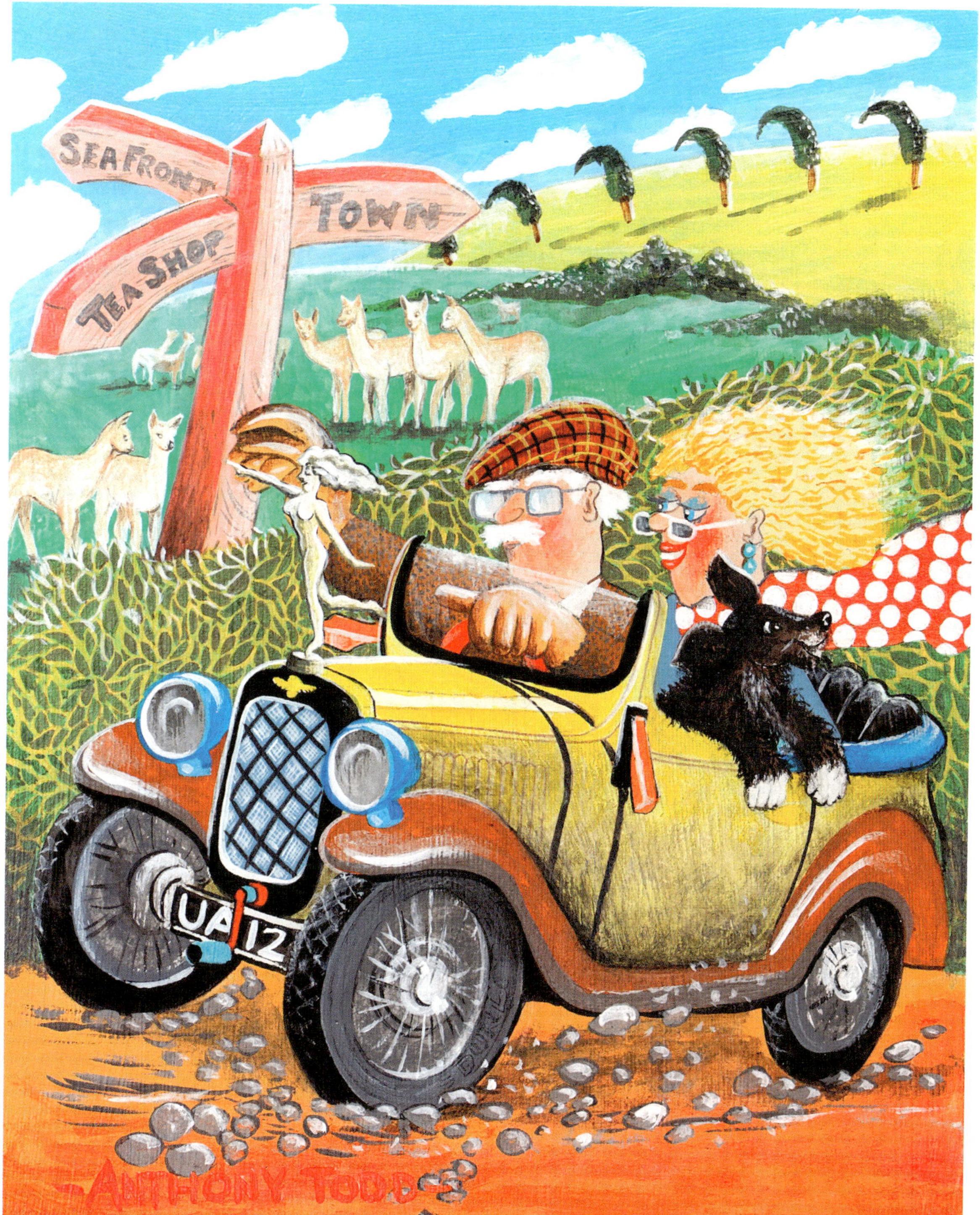
SEA FRONT
TOWN
TEA SHOP
UA 12
ANTHONY TODD

Up The City!

Dotty and Amanda don't know much about football but they like watching the local team with Uncle Albert. He's not keen, they spend the whole match shouting and screaming in his ear, but he says nothing.

They always buy him his Bovril and sausage roll at half-time. He feels it's best to keep quiet otherwise he could starve to death! He would never pay what they're asking for a mangy sausage roll; but of course if they are on offer….

Amanda is in love with the Number Nine, Roger Sugar. She thinks he is a real sweetie. She says "His thighs are like tree trunks and he has such lovely hair." Dotty sniffs and tells her she should be ashamed of herself at her age.

Uncle Albert burps loudly, as the sausage roll decides to give his stomach something else to think about!

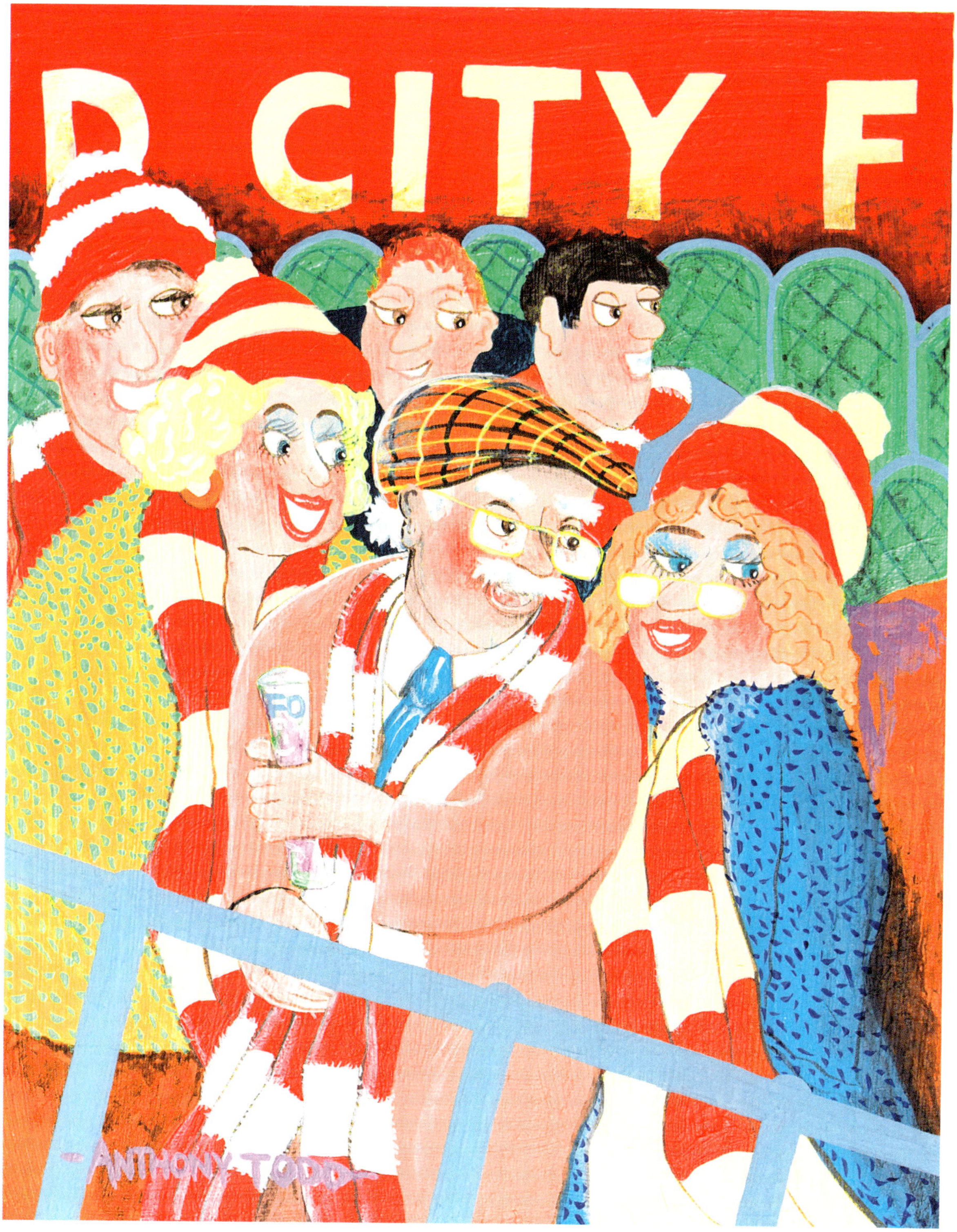
D CITY F
ANTHONY TODD

Honeysuckle Rose and a Soggy Sponge

Amanda has always been good with her hands, and when Uncle Albert mentioned his shoulders were playing up, she duly obliged with her Honeysuckle Rose soap.

Up to his elbows in bubbles, Uncle Albert sits in the bath. Amanda splashes in beside him, soap in one hand and a sponge scrub in the other. Uncle Albert doesn't like Honeysuckle Rose soap. He shuts his eyes tightly, not daring to look, and thinks of his allotment.

"I wonder if I should grow curly kale or sprouts?" he forces himself to think. Amanda squeezes the suds-filled sponge gently over his neck and chest. "No, it will have to be those giant onions, or maybe a few sticks of rhubarb."

Suddenly Uncle Albert likes Honeysuckle Rose soap very much indeed!

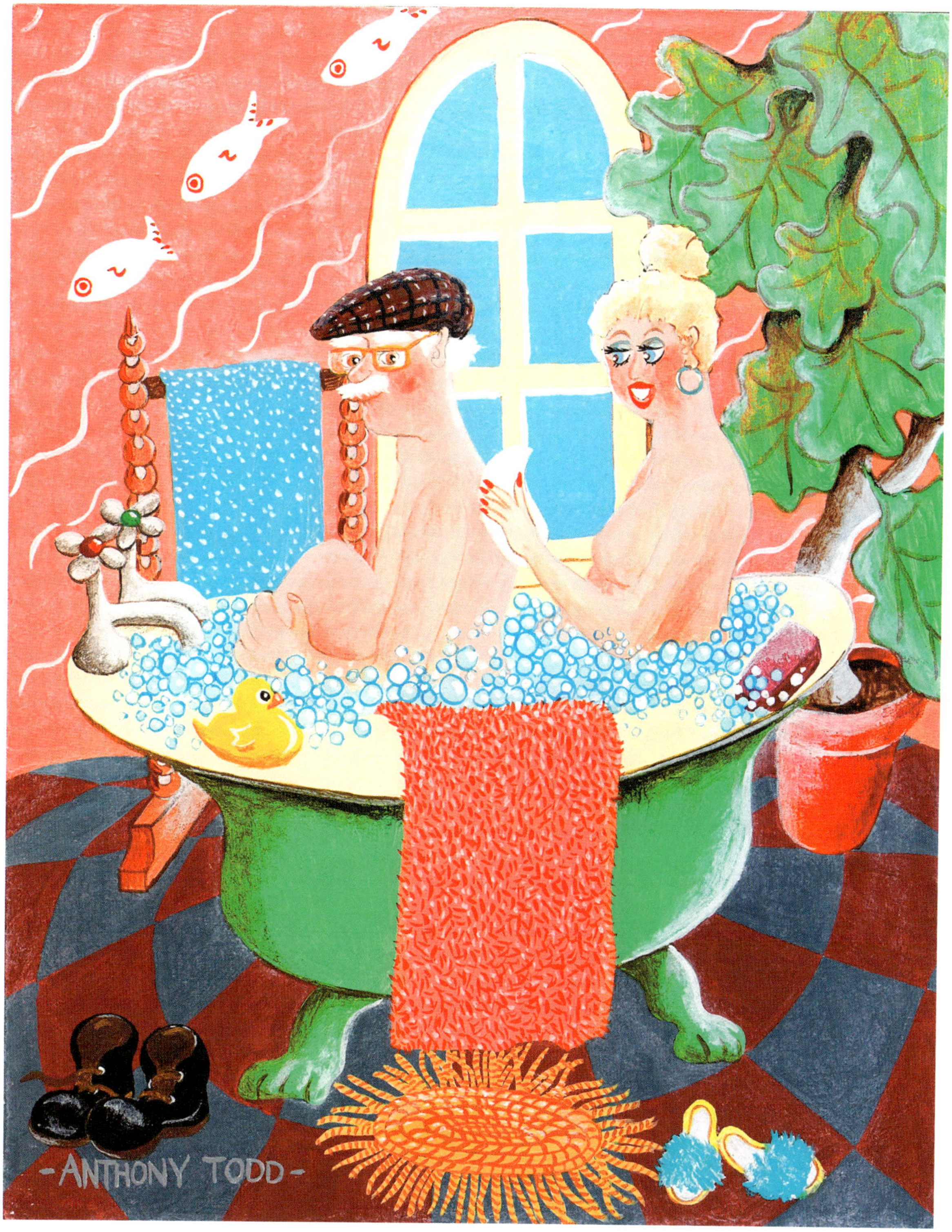
-ANTHONY TODD-

Ice Cream for Three

Brenda and Amanda enjoy ice cream but what they really enjoy is a good old gossip.

They send Uncle Albert off to do his shark fishing, or whatever he does, and they natter on about more important things. Usually they talk about the latest films showing at the Gaumont.

Sometimes they talk about Troy, the dishy assistant in the Regal coffee shop. Since he first started at the Regal, both Brenda and Amanda have drunk more than their fair share of coffee - and Amanda doesn't even like coffee!
She says she goes there for the 'ambience'. Brenda says she doesn't know what that means; she thinks it's something to do with Troy's pert bottom.

Amanda tells her not to be so personal!

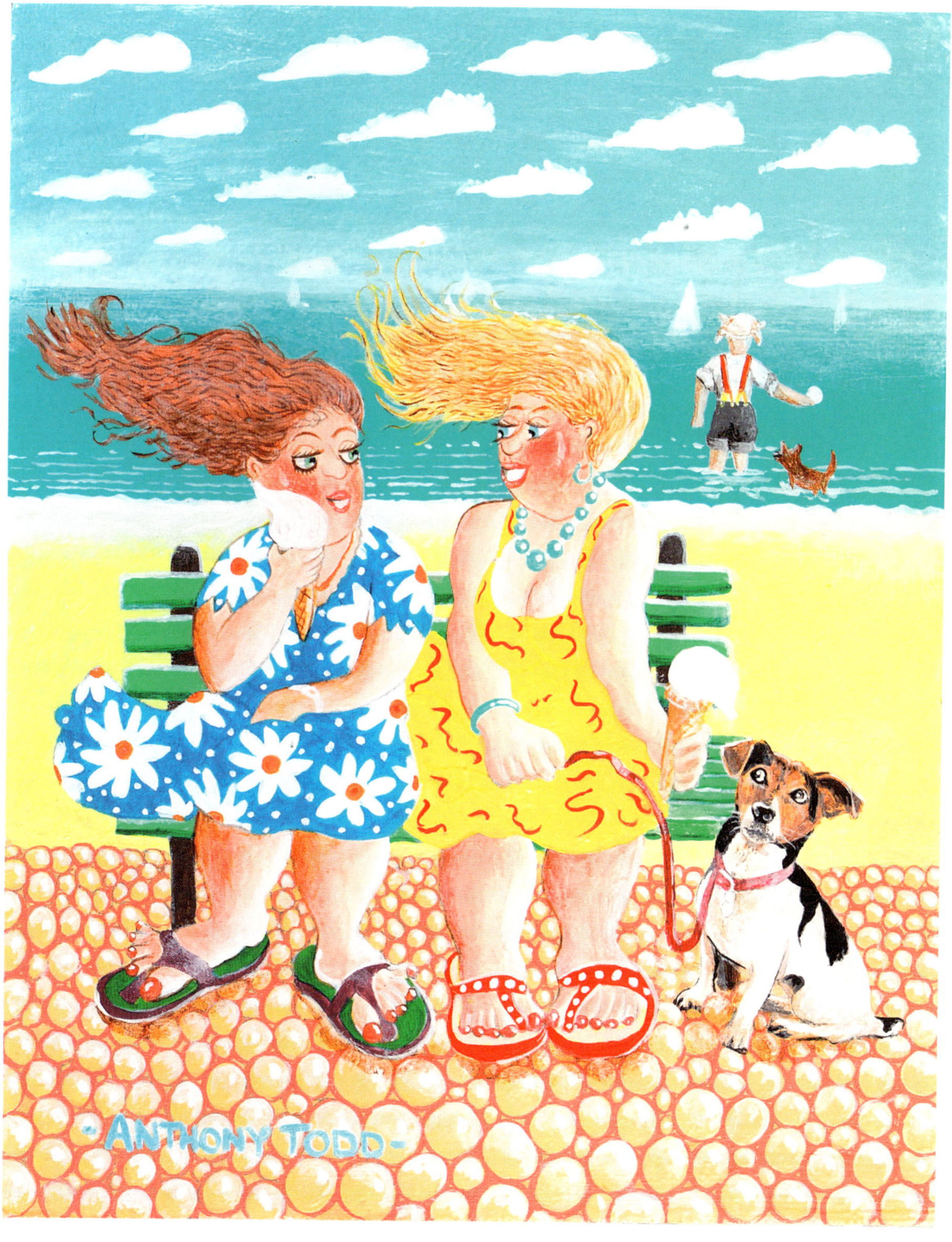
-ANTHONY TODD-

The Office

Uncle Albert spends a lot of time in his shed. He uses it as his office and likes to lounge in his rocking chair and listen to football matches on his DABS radio.

He sits there for ages, with his Daily Mirror spread out, and studies his Tesco shares wondering whether he can still afford to live in luxury. He keeps a nice selection of Tesco's red wine and some bottles of Dancing Dave's Turnip and Carrot sparkling Champagne in the corner behind the compost bags. Dancing Dave swears it should be drunk straightaway, but Rupert, who works at the Off Licence, says he would leave it well alone. It certainly looks lethal.

Uncle Albert thinks he may let it mature for a few years. He likes a nice vintage Champagne!

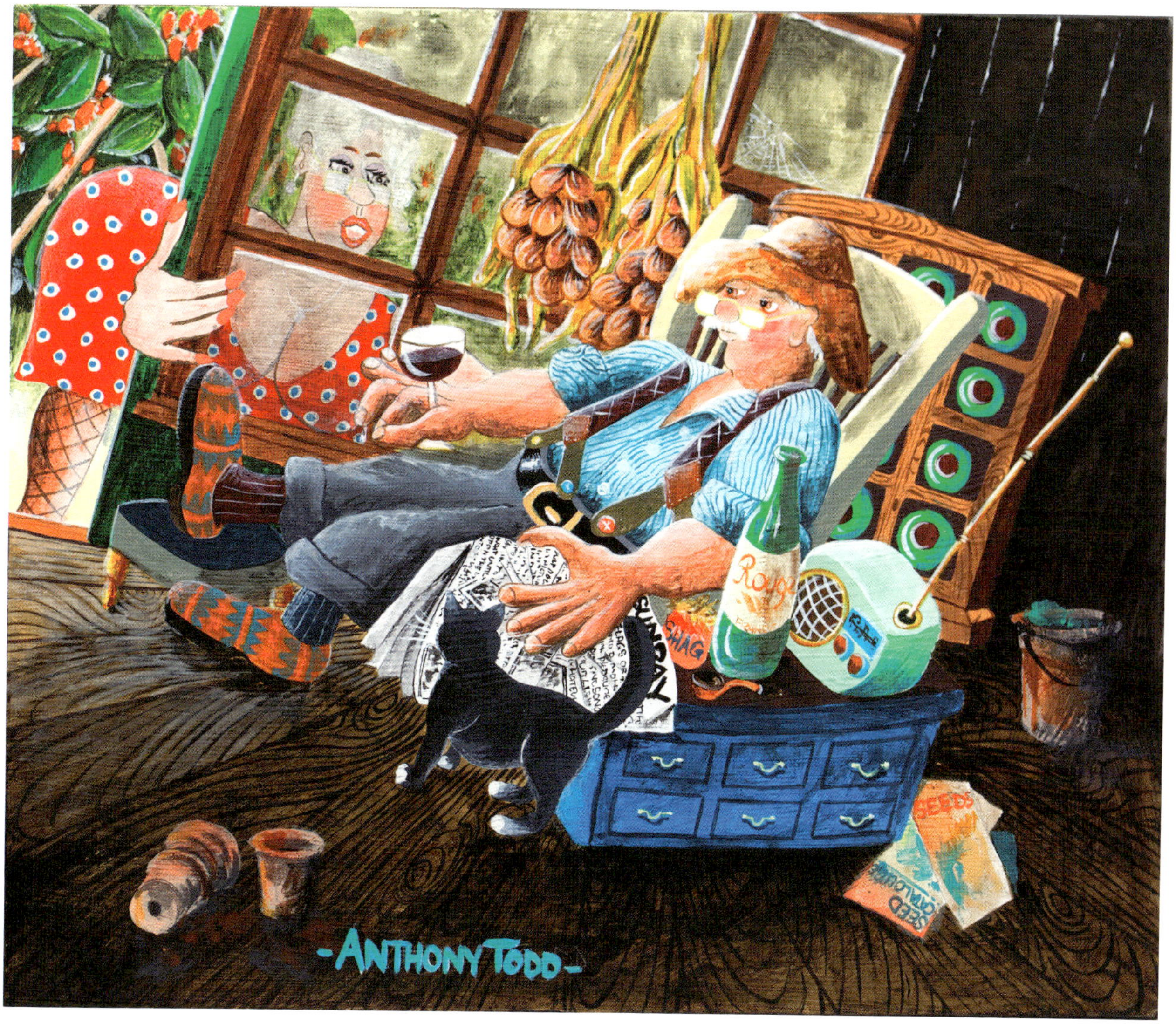
Rouge
SHAG
SEEDS
SEED CATALOGUE
-ANTHONY TODD-

A Visit to the Mango-Calypso Bar

Brenda introduces Uncle Albert to the Mango-Calypso Bar. They sit, wearing tropical shirts, sipping countless cocktails. Brenda soon gets giggly and feels quite seasick. She looses count after five Skegness Sunsets (a very strong cocktail which comes with spinning umbrellas and floating seaweed). She says just the sight of a Skegness Sunset puts her in mind of a very choppy North Sea ferry crossing.

After just four Sweating Monks, Uncle Albert burps and decides they taste a bit like Watneys Red Barrel and he gets a touch homesick for The Butchers Arms.

When he asks for a small beer a heavy set man, with a ponytail and a ragged scar, asks them both to leave for being drunk.

"I'd rather have a Chinese than any more of that foreign rubbish", Uncle Albert slurs, as they tiptoe out of The Mango-Calypso bar.

Brenda tells him not to be so silly.

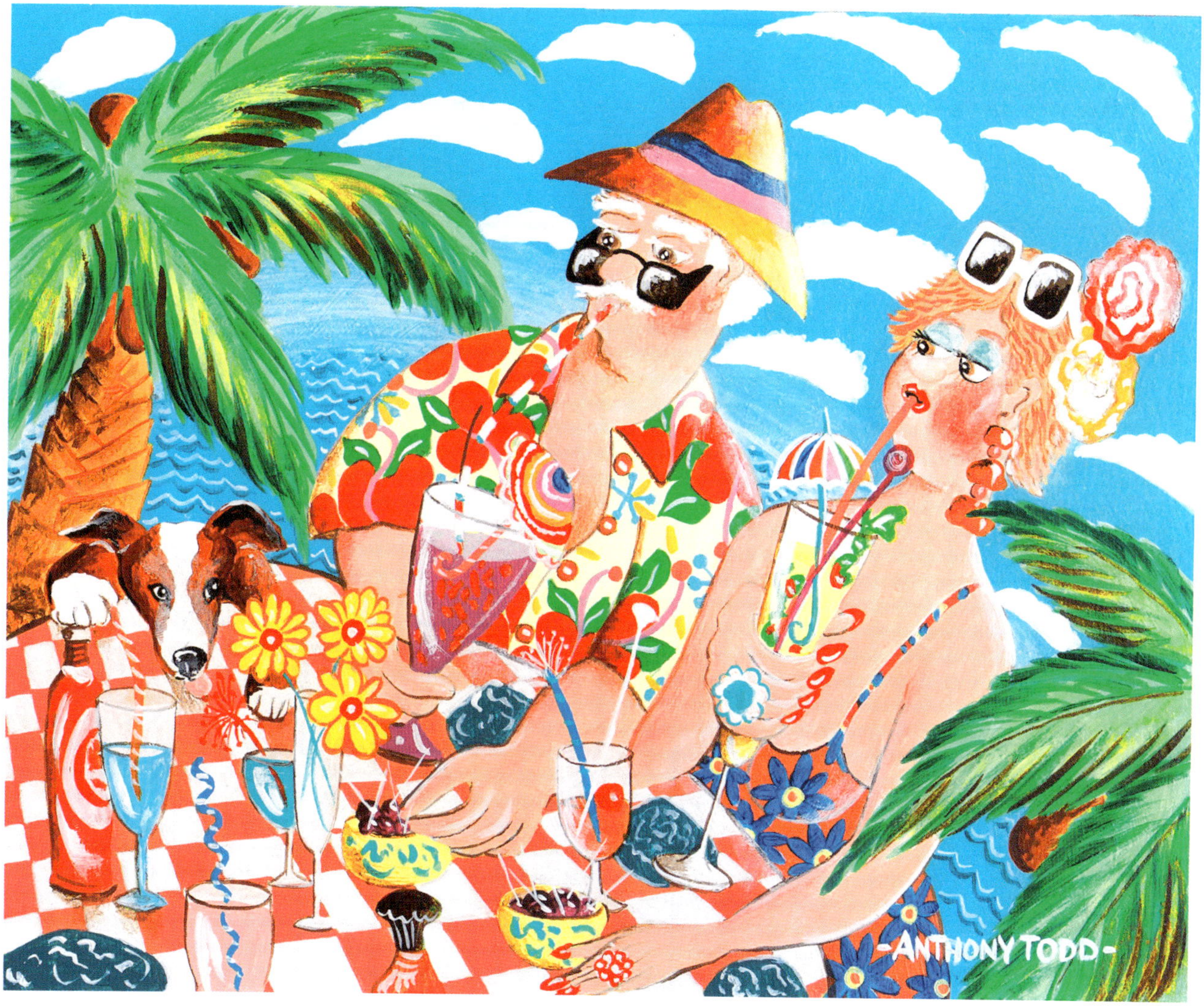
-ANTHONY TODD-

Uncle Albert's Birthday Lunch

Making a Day of It

The sun rises over the tall hedge at the bottom of the allotment. "It's going to be one of those hot and humid days", murmurs Uncle Albert, as he idly stirs his tea with a plastic seed label.

Today is his big, special birthday and most of the villagers are coming up to the allotment for lunch to celebrate, and Dotty, Amanda and Brenda have arranged for everyone to bring chairs, food and drink.

"Make a day of it", cries Brenda as tables arrive from the Village Hall, and soon every available space is covered on Uncle Albert's allotment.

The red and white checked tablecloths gleam in the morning sun, and by noon the tables are beginning to groan under the weight of food and bottles, as Uncle Albert's friends arrive with their chairs, hampers and sun-umbrellas.

Groups sit around tables, bottles are uncorked and the party begins.

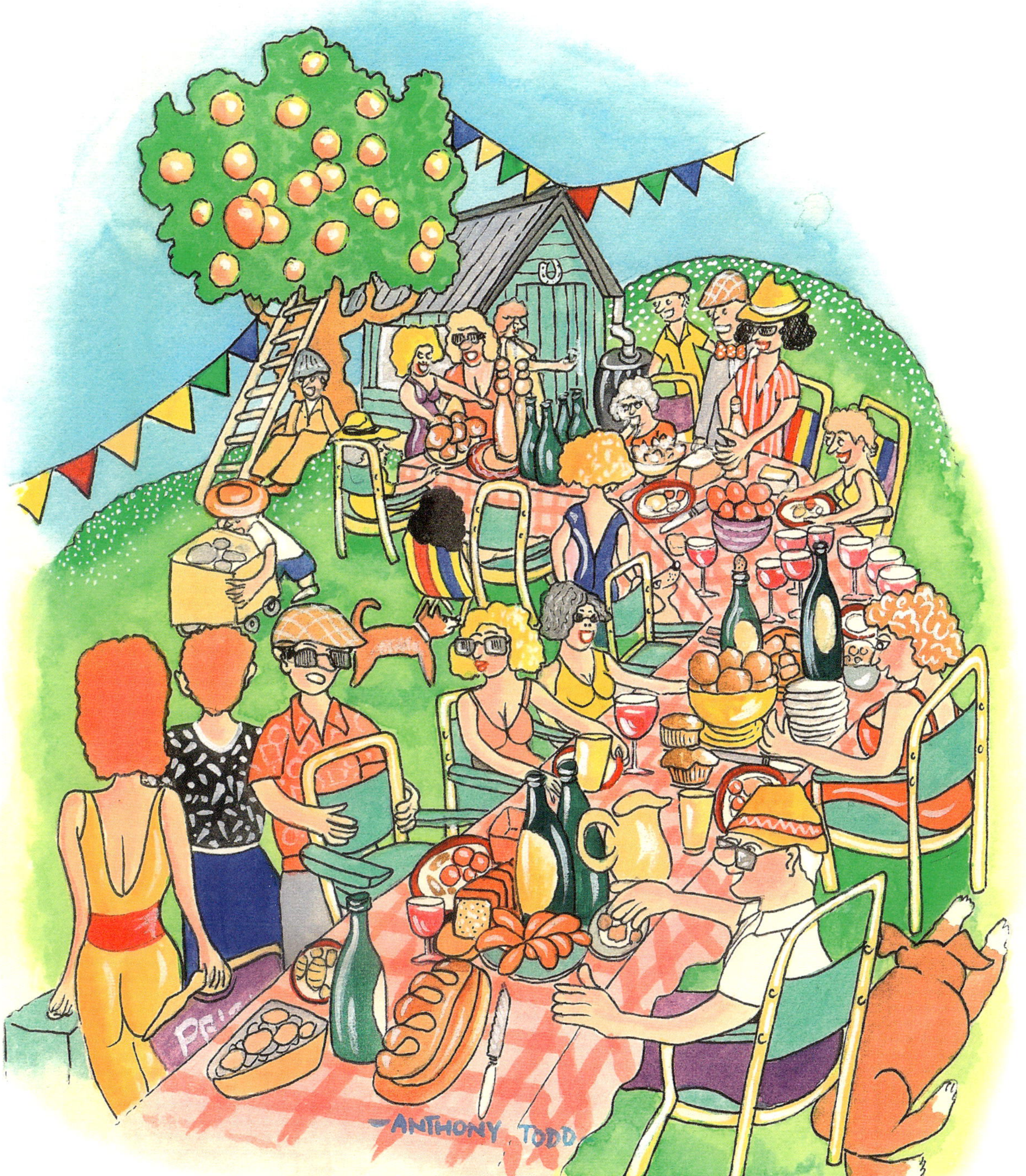
ANTHONY TODD

Uncle Albert's Birthday Lunch

Fluttering Eyelashes and Thrusting Bosoms

Miss Crisp, the Dog Show judge, flutters her new Super Long Eyelashes and sits up close to Micky Finn, the fishmonger. He runs the wet fish shop in the High Street, and reckons his crabs are the best in England.

Miss Crisp lovingly feeds him some of her freshly baked Gypsy Cream biscuits by hand, her crimson nail varnish glinting in the sun. In reply he passes her one of his Marmite and sardine sandwiches, which have started to curl up in the heat of the midday sun. He devours the biscuits much like a seal swallowing fish from his keeper, smacking his rubbery lips loudly. He cannot keep his eyes off her yellow, low-cut dress which accentuates her thrusting bosom.

Their short romance has been a secret, and he hopes nobody notices their subtle body language, as under the table, he gently squeezes her stocking-clad knee.

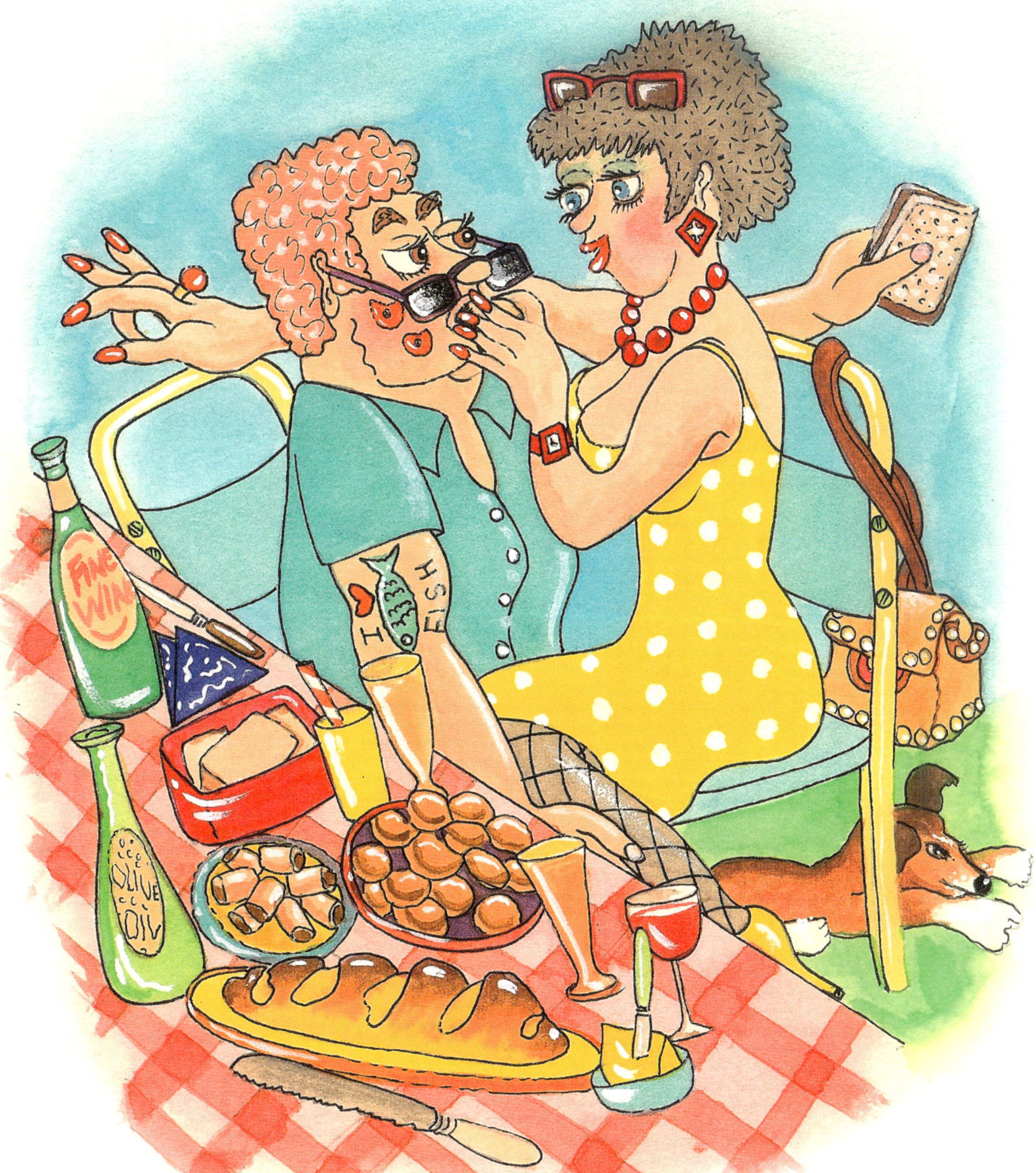
FINE WIN
I ♥ FISH

Uncle Albert's Birthday Lunch

Posh Champagne and Sunglasses

Dancing Dave has brought four dozen bottles of his best Carrot and Turnip Vintage Champagne to Uncle Albert's birthday lunch.

The bottles have been lying in straw, in his outside loo, for nearly two years to mature, and should be at their very best by now.

He and Quickstep Chris tried a bottle or two last night, and both are now wearing sunglasses and clutching their heads.

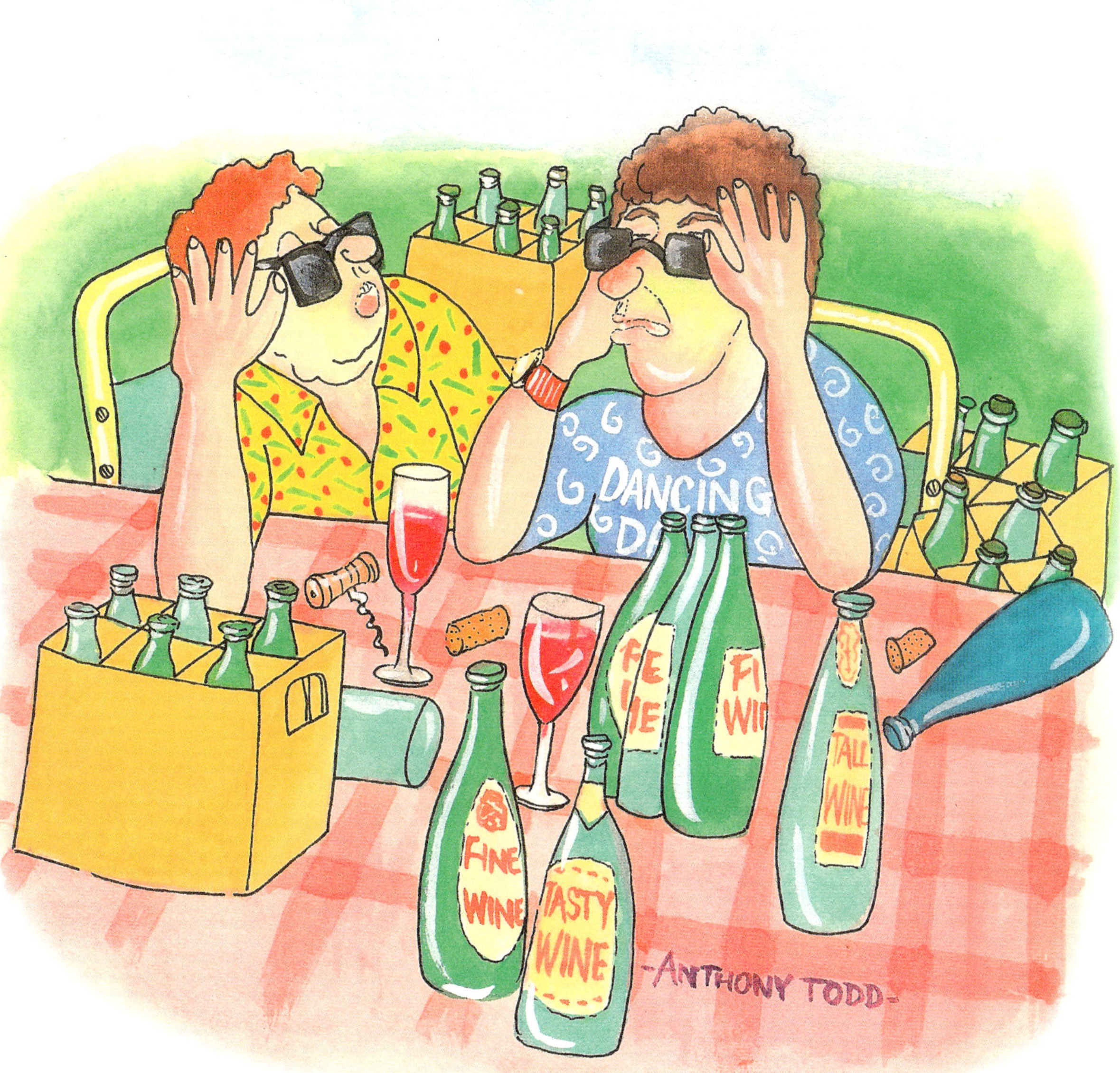
DANCING
FINE WINE
TASTY WINE
-ANTHONY TODD-

Uncle Albert's Birthday Lunch

Spike and Dusty Hoover Up

Spike and Dusty, Uncle Albert's pooches, vie for the best food spots under the tables. They loiter next to Billy Boothright, who has always been a messy eater.

As chunks of his mother's home baked rabbit and gravy pie escape his mouth, they are snapped up in mid-air by whichever dog is nearest, or quickest. Not one piece of pie reaches the ground.

After a while, when Billy's chomping slows down to a half-hearted chew, the pooches move on to better spots further along the tables.

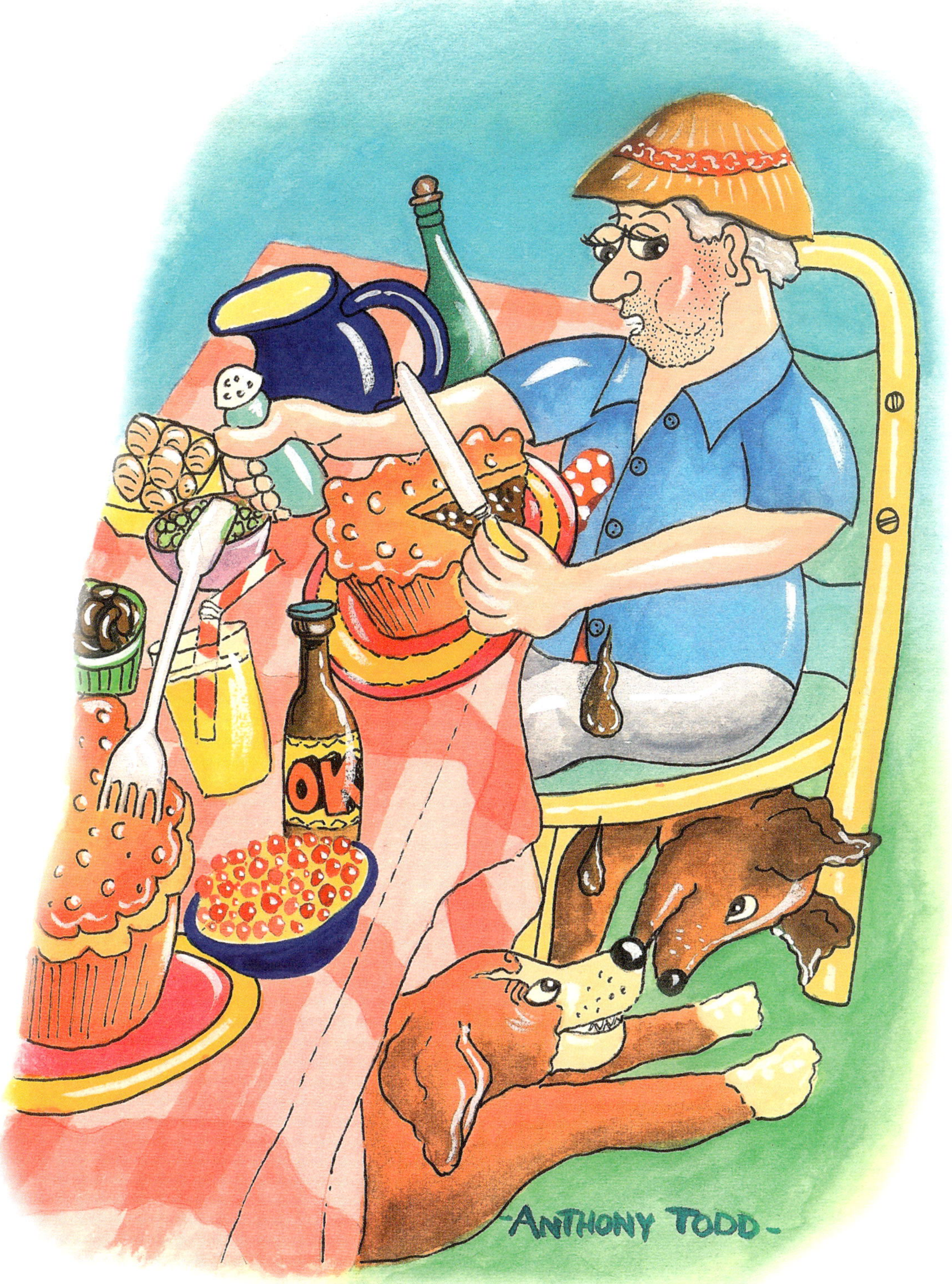
OK
-ANTHONY TODD-

Uncle Albert's Birthday Lunch

Let's See Your Thong, Troy

Brenda has got on her skimpiest sun-dress. She has heard that Troy, the dishy assistant from the Regal Coffee Shop, might come along to the party this afternoon.

She denies that she is in love with Troy…. but she does fancy him…. a lot. "He's such a good looking boy", she murmurs, as she conjures up a dazzling image of Troy posing in his thong, and very little else. She breaks out in a vivid rash, which she has more than once blamed on the fierceness of the sun!

Dabbing her face and throat with a silk scarf, she stares at the picket gate at the far end of the allotment, willing Troy to make a spectacular entrance. She can hardly believe her eyes when Troy suddenly appears, dressed, not in a thong, but in a colourful shirt and light trousers. She slams her Ray-Burns onto the end of her nose, licks her lips and rushes to him with arms outstretched. (She saw this being done once in a chocolate ad and thinks it looks cool.)

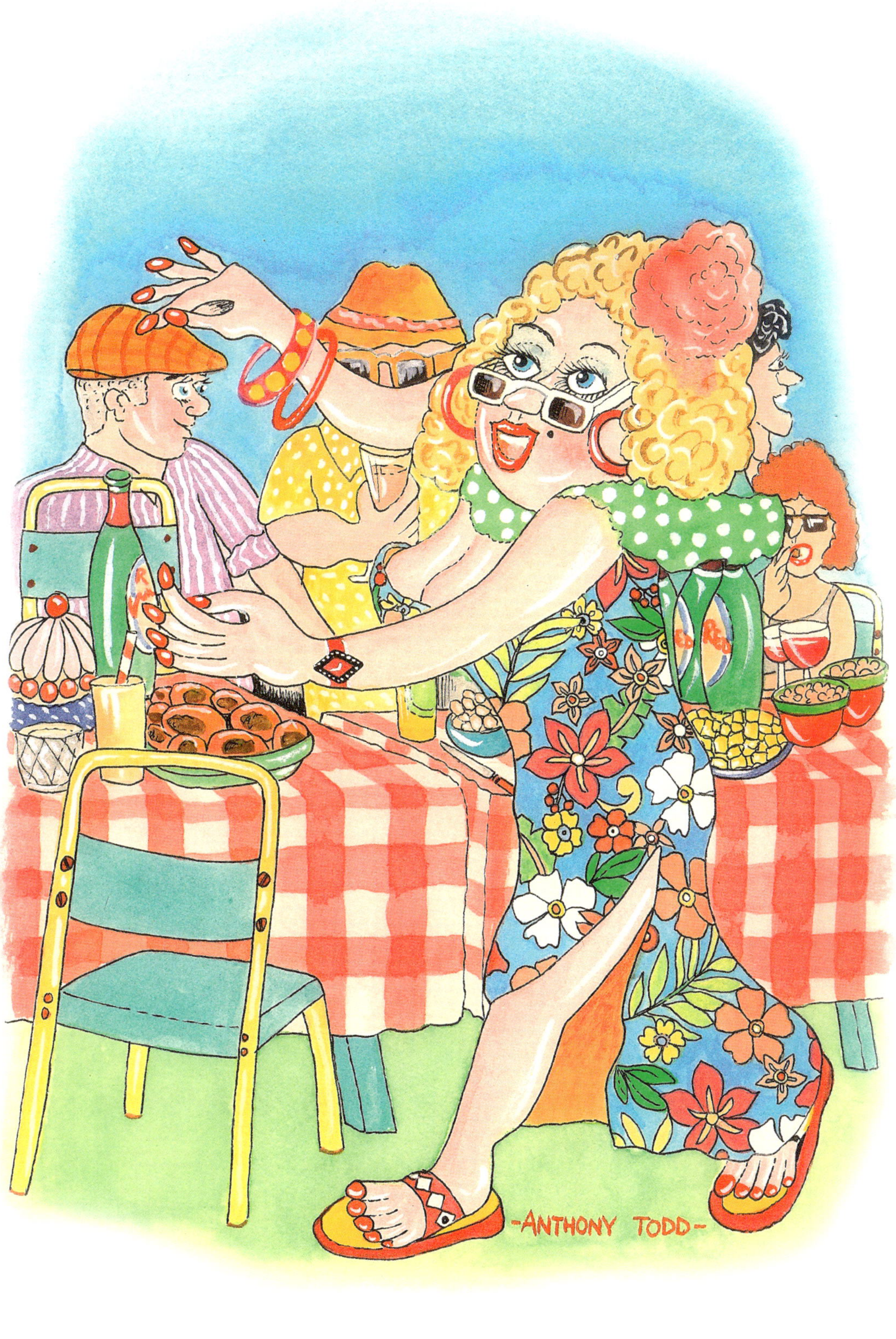
-ANTHONY TODD-

"**Troy darling,** how lovely to see you!" she gushes. "Hello Brenda," Troy replies "meet Julian, my partner." Troy pushes forward a good looking young man, and Brenda, looking stunned, limply shakes his hand. "Ooh..er", she mumbles, "I didn't know."

"**Didn't know what?**" laughs Troy. "That I didn't have a male partner? Everyone else seems to know about it, and really, does it matter that much anyway?" "Of course not", stammers Brenda, "I knew all along, I was only saying to Amanda yesterday what a lovely couple you make."

Troy and Julian laugh with joy as Brenda wiggles off with her nose in the air, glaring at everyone she passes.

Uncle Albert's Birthday Lunch

The Goose and the Traffic Cone

Rupert, captain of the Bowls Club and recent manager of Stiff & Partners, the High Street undertakers, sits at the end table by himself. He sips his pint of mild slowly, peering over his glasses at the, almost empty, paddock bordering the allotments - almost empty, but not quite. Rupert smiles as he catches sight of a white goose standing next to a red and white, striped traffic cone.

Some years ago a pair of geese occupied the field, they would fly away and return every spring without fail; it was their home. Children fed them every day and soon the village adopted the pair. Rupert, who owned the field, kept the paddock empty for the geese to return to every year. He loved seeing them fly in, honking and flapping noisily from their journey away.

Then last year only one of the geese returned. It looked lonely by itself in the paddock and spent the next few weeks waddling from one end to the other, as if looking for its partner. It refused food, and as the days went by began to look more and more dirty and dejected. Everyone became worried and expected the worst. Then, one morning, Rupert looked over the hedge and instead of seeing a sad looking goose, saw a red and white, striped traffic cone in the middle of the field. Standing beside it was the goose, looking very spritely, feeding away happily from a pile of food left by the children.

Someone had thrown the cone into the field as a prank. Rupert thought that perhaps the poor goose had poor vision and assumed its partner had returned. The goose fed well and looked extremely happy. Then one morning it took off, circled the village with a loud honking…. and flew off into the mist.

No one really expected to see the bird again. "That's the last we will see of your goose", uttered Jonnie Rotten to Rupert, as they stood looking into the sky several months later. "They mate for life you see, so some old traffic cone isn't going to entice it back." "We'll see," said Rupert "I'm going to leave the cone in the field just in case, you never know, it just might return."

Days later a loud honking and hooting greeted the quietness of the countryside. Looking up, villagers saw the white goose come swooping into the paddock….. to land just inches from the traffic cone. The goose had returned! The news of the returning goose caused great excitement and happiness around the village.

The happiest person of all was Rupert, captain of the Bowls Club and recent manager of Stiff & Partners, the High Street undertakers… and proud goose owner.

The goose flies away and returns every year, back to the friendly, red and white traffic cone.

The above is a true story.

Uncle Albert's Birthday Lunch
Squeak, Squeak, Squeak

Arthur Crown sips his frothy shandy from a tall glass and leans back in his chair. He surveys the crowded scene; everyone seems to be enjoying themselves at Uncle Albert's party.

All his friends call him 'Arfer', as in 'arfer-crown'. He used to be known as 'Squeaker Crown' because the wheel on his barrow developed a high pitched squeak. On each revolution of the wheel, it would emit a loud squeak that could be heard all over the allotments. Squeaker liked the loud noise, he would creep up behind his mates and they would have to leap out of the way when they heard the dreaded 'squeak, squeak, squeak, squeak' of the barrow. Of course, the faster he went, the quicker the squeaks. Some of his friends found it all a bit too much and the squeaking and squealing got on their nerves.

One day, Monty, who hated the sight of Squeaker and his barrow, decided he had had enough and drenched the offending wheel in oil. The squeaking disappeared and Squeaker was very annoyed.

In a rage, he shouted at Monty "What did you go and do that for? I've got no idea how fast I'm going now!"

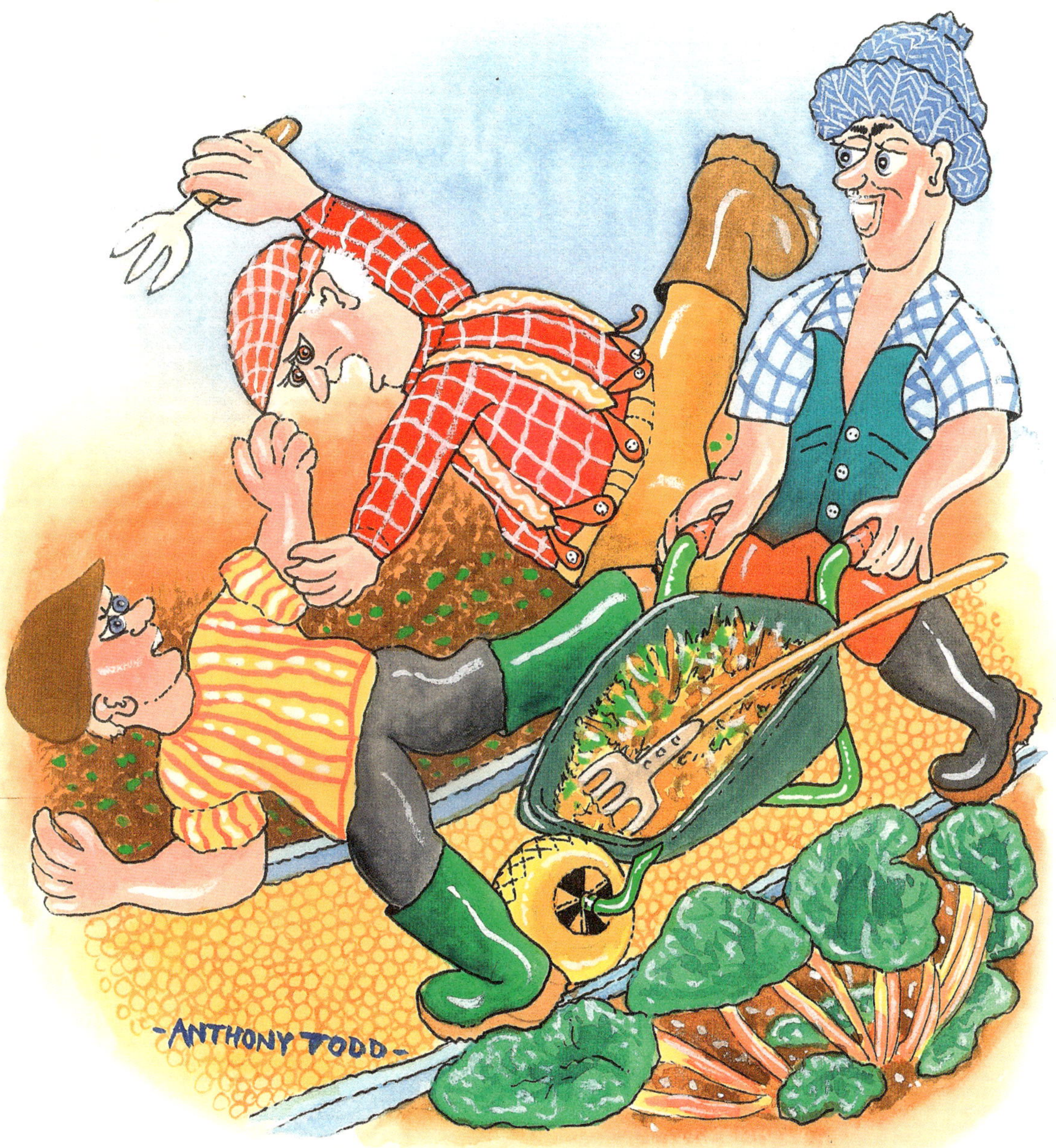
-ANTHONY TODD-

Uncle Albert's Birthday Lunch

Absolute Nectar

George and Phil sit, with Uncle Albert at the next table, sipping glasses of ice cold cider. Uncle Albert and George supply the apples from their allotments and Phil bottles up the amber liquid. They have several dozen bottles to consume between them, so they don't talk a lot, they just sip.

Last year was a particularly good year for apples and Phil won the Challenge Shield for his cider. But he did not win entirely by good luck alone. It was late on a Thursday evening when Phil, who had been sampling some cider in his garage, switched the lights off and went to bed.

Next morning he found he had not turned the cider barrel tap fully off, and only a quarter of the precious stuff was left, certainly not enough to impress the judges at the fair. In desperation, he decided the only thing he could do was to make a visit to the local Tesco store.

It took seventeen large bottles of Premium Cider to top up the barrel, and when Phil tasted the result he was amazed.

"ABSOLUTE NECTAR!!!"

"**You could** bottle this stuff and sell it to Tesco," said George "it's as good as their Premium Cider any day."

Phil sat at the table and said nothing, but thought he must remember to get rid of the evidence and go to the bottle bank the next morning, with his seventeen empty Tesco Premium Cider bottles!

No Crab for Me

"I'm taking it home for my tea", grins Uncle Albert, holding up a tiny crab he had found on the sand. "Don't you bring that thing near me!" screams Brenda, running up the beach.

She hates crabs, either swimming around in the sea or upside down in a sandwich. She thinks they are horrible. She swears one moved on the wet fish counter in the High Street, and told the fishmonger about it. "No, they are all dead as a doorknob", laughed the fishmonger with glee. Not convinced, she stared at the crab for some time, and was totally freaked out when it opened one eye and winked at her!

Brenda refuses to speak to the fishmonger now, even if his haddock is half price!

- ANTHONY TODD -

In the Sack with Amanda

Amanda and Uncle Albert win the sack race at the village fete. Uncle Albert says he thought he saw a mouse in the sack, this was to make Amanda hop faster....and they won in record time! He reckons such a great victory is down to good living and dedicated team work.

Uncle Albert however did not do quite so well in the 100 yard dash. The first-aid team, a large girl and her asthmatic aunt, found it impossible to get him back on his feet, just fifteen yards down the track. Albert reckons his veins let him down at the last moment. Amanda thinks he forgot to take his tablets and that he should take more roughage with his cornflakes.

Uncle Albert is thinking of giving up running sports and may take up ferret breeding instead.

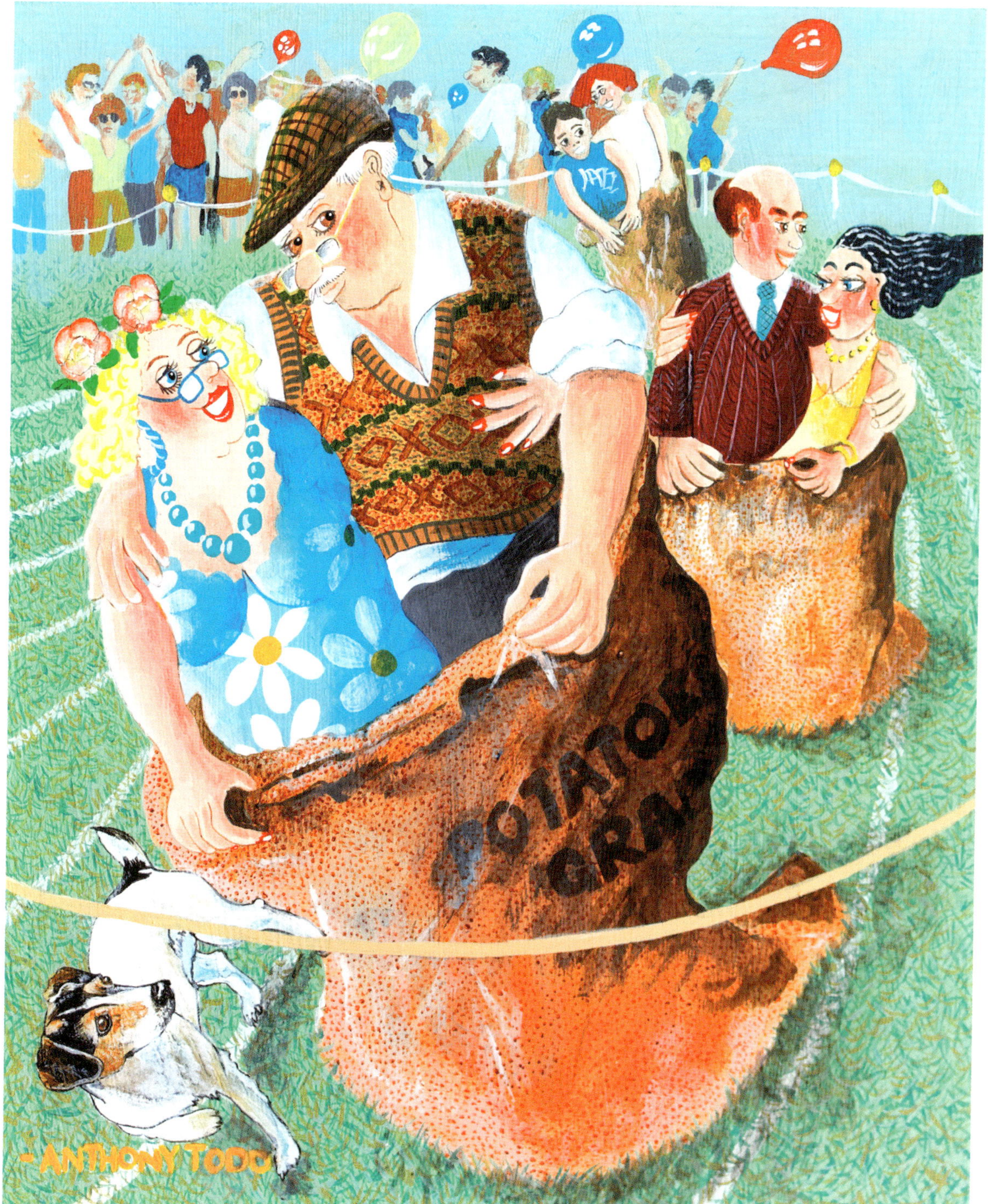

I Hate Gulls

A day at the seaside with Brenda is always something to look forward to, thinks Uncle Albert. Brenda always pays for the deckchairs and brings a wonderful picnic, packed in her large, red bag.

She looks a treat in her mock Ray-Burn sunglasses, which bounce up and down on the end of her nose as she snores, loudly.

Seagulls tend to veer away from Brenda; they hate the sound of snoring. Instead, they normally make for Uncle Albert's spotted handkerchief, which he uses to keep the sun off his head. When they attack it, Uncle Albert yells and waves his arms around, but they seem to enjoy this and soon there are ten or so seagulls swooping and wheeling around Uncle Albert's bright red headwear.

Uncle Albert hates seagulls!

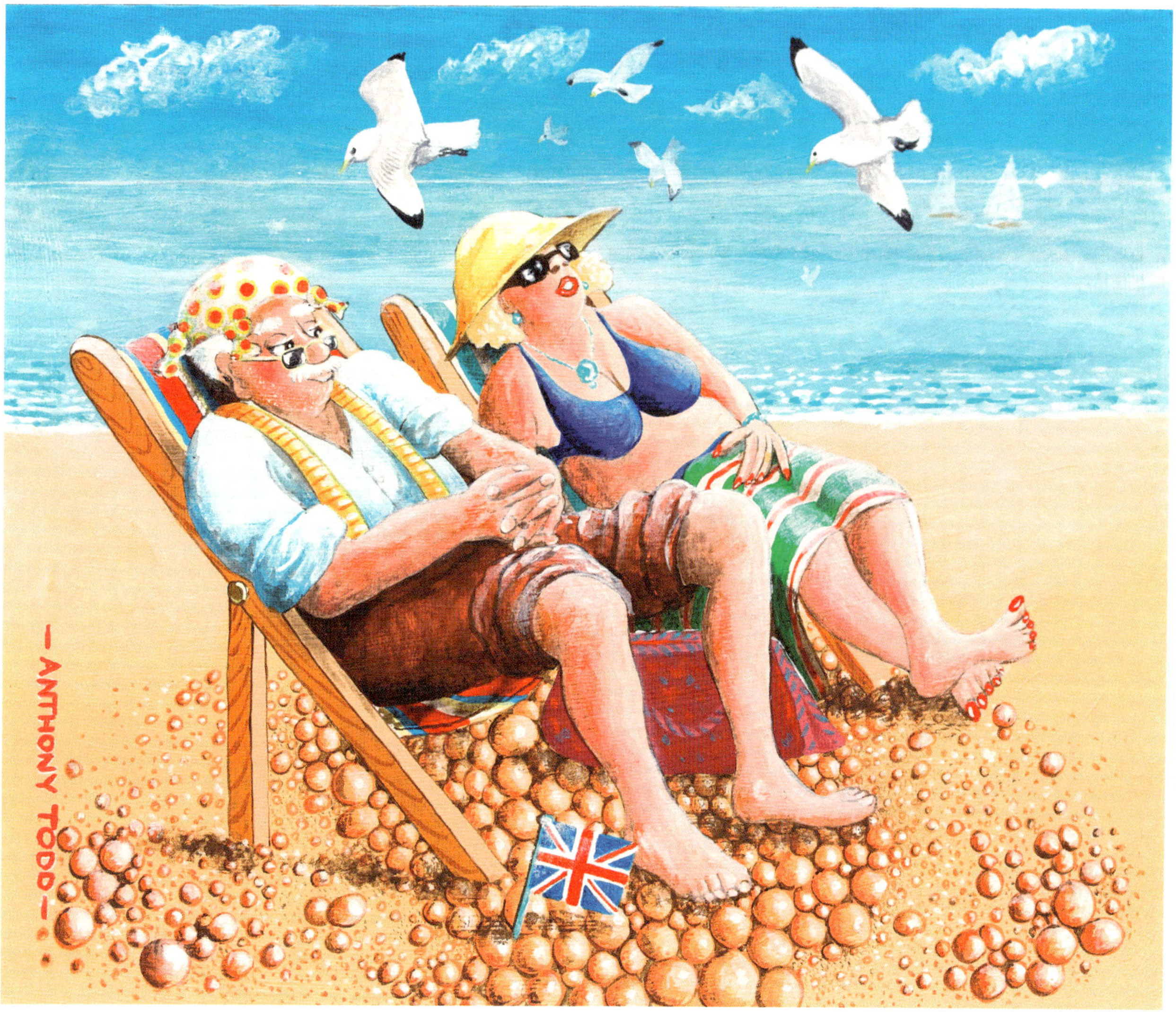

- ANTHONY TODD -

A Night Out at the Plaza Ballroom

Uncle Albert can dance a mean quickstep. He always wears a suit when he takes Amanda to the Plaza Ballroom. It was originally Bill Boothright's demob suit, so it's seen a few years. Billy could not wait to get rid of it, as it never did fit him. The arms and legs were four inches too long for him.

The suit fits Uncle Albert a real treat; worth every penny of the lame ferret he exchanged for it, especially as the ferret died the very next day!

Amanda and Albert often find they are the only ones dancing. Quickstep Chris, who plays the trombone, says it's the rank smell of mothballs from Uncle Albert's suit that puts the other dancers off.

Amanda, who has always had a touch of sinus trouble, sniffs the air and thinks maybe it's not his aftershave after all.

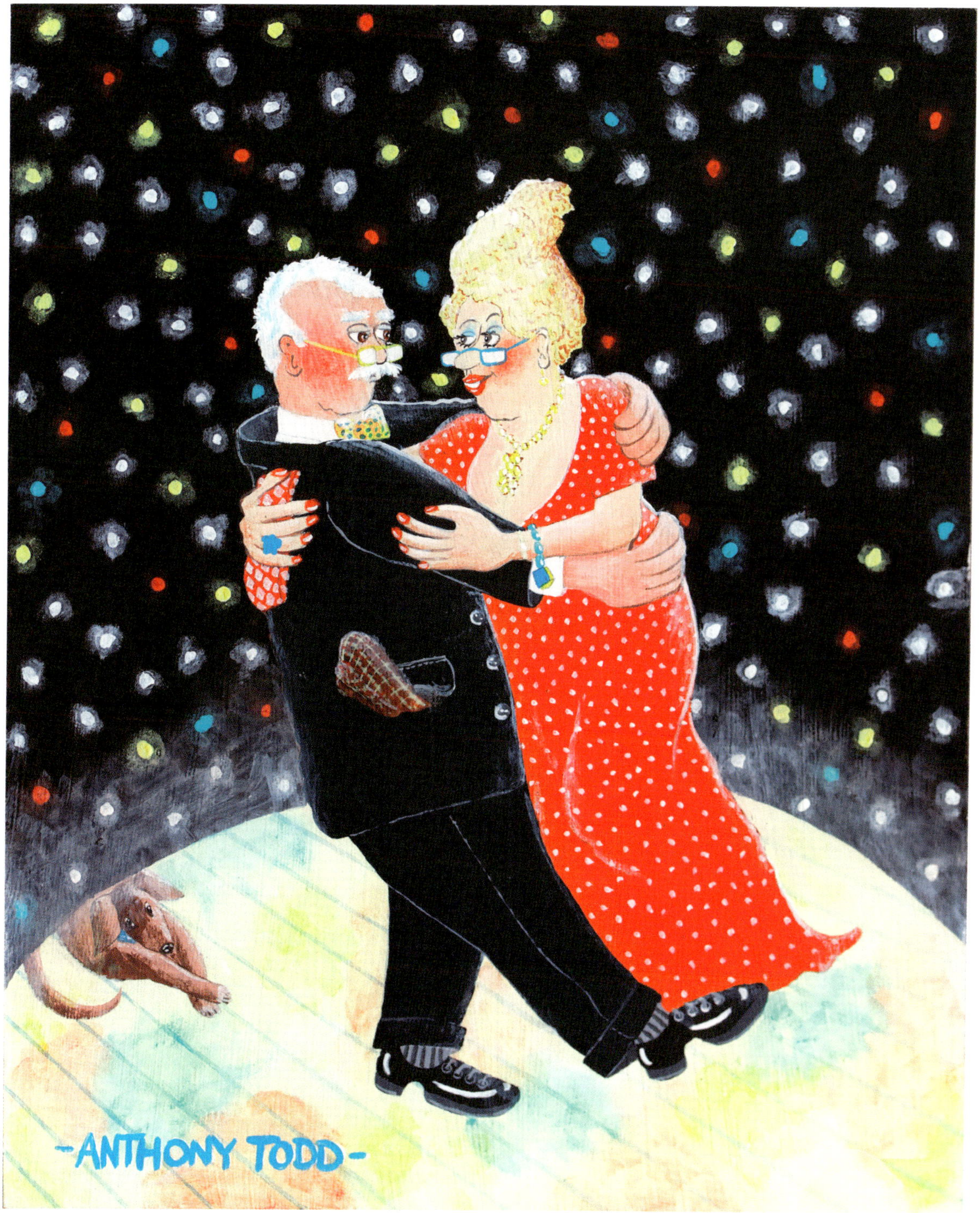
-ANTHONY TODD-

In The Butchers Arms

Uncle Albert and the girls meet at The Butchers Arms for a quick drink before the match. They wear their red and white scarves, talk tactics and forecast the final score. Dotty always guesses the final score correctly.

One Saturday, the score ended up fifteen-nil and Dotty was, as usual, spot on. Everyone thinks she is amazing. Dotty knows she will forecast it wrong one week, because she admits she knows nothing about football but so far she has been very lucky.

Uncle Albert thinks girls should not go to football matches, but he never says anything. After all, they always buy the beer and crisps. He has been known to choke on his beer when one of the girls starts on about the offside rule, or about how good looking the opposing goalkeeper is, with his dark, glossy hair and flashing eyes.

He thinks he would be better off watching ladies' Beach Ball; but he doesn't think his heart would stand up to it!

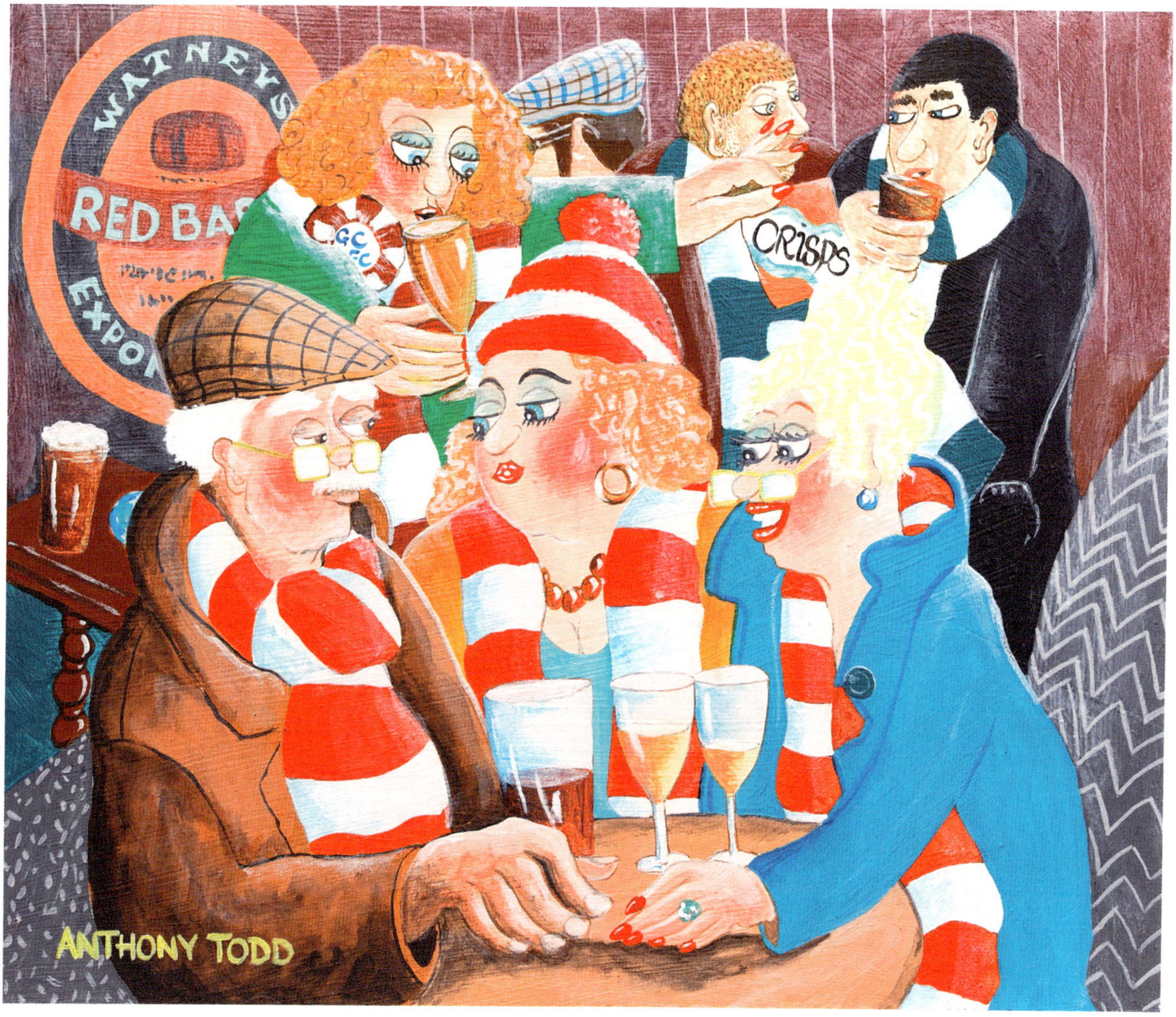
WATNEYS
CRISPS
ANTHONY TODD

Up, Up and Away

There is nothing like a colourful kite skipping above the white fluffy clouds, muses Brenda, as Uncle Albert gets his Rainbow Warrior airborne. "What a sight!" he yells, as the kite soars up,up .... and straight down with a mighty crash - splinters flying everywhere.

"Ooh what happened?" cries a distressed Brenda, eying up the tangled heap. "Bad workmanship" snaps Uncle Albert, fielding the blame slightly. His flying skills are not as honed as they should be. He insists that "it's all down to the foreign rubbish flooding the country". Brenda watches, as several Rainbow Warriors weave in and out among the clouds, tugged this way and that by small, excited children.

"I never did like kite flying", moans Uncle Albert, as he kicks a stone in the air.

Brenda thinks he should attend an anger management course.

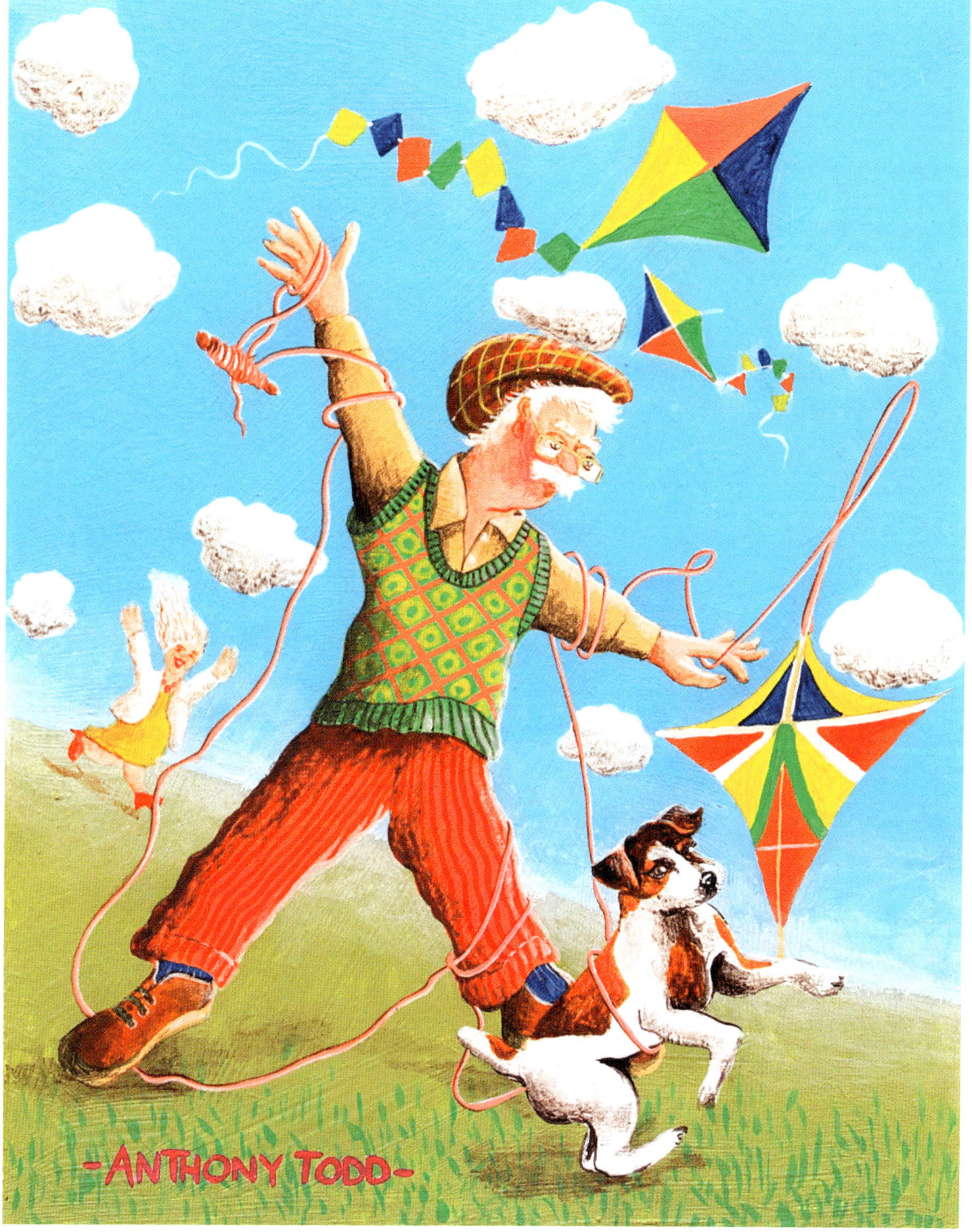
-ANTHONY TODD-

Best Leeks in Show

Uncle Albert cannot believe his leeks have won 'Best in Show'. "All those months of pampering were well worth it", he says, as he raises the large, silver cup for all to see.

"Well done!" cry Dotty, Amanda and Brenda, clapping their hands and squealing loudly. George and Phil, both past champions, sniff and offer stunted congratulations. "Super!" says the judge "Best I've ever seen", hoping he will be invited to a champion leek and chicken pie supper, washed down with a glass or two of Dancing Dave's Turnip and Carrot Sparkling Champagne.

"Best day of my life", sniffles Uncle Albert, overcome by it all, suddenly feeling guilty that he had purchased the 'winning leeks' from Rosie's Fruit & Veg stall that very morning.

-ANTHONY TODD-

Uncle Albert Takes Brenda Out

Occasionally Uncle Albert enjoys taking Brenda out in his Austin Seven, a very smart car in its day.

In fine weather he puts the roof down, because he feels Brenda quite likes to pose in her mock Ray-Burns, pursing her highly glossed lips to all and sundry. The sun plays havoc with Uncle Albert's bald patch, so he is forced to wear his tweed 'cheese cutter' cap. Brenda doesn't mind, she often says how dapper he looks, especially when his cap is set at a jaunty angle and how much he looks like Clint Eastwood in those films.

Brenda is very good at changing tyres; the odd puncture can often give Uncle Albert time to browse the paper and check his Tesco shares, while Brenda heaves a wheel off and replaces it with a spare from the boot.

On really fine days, Uncle Albert speeds along, with his sleeves rolled up and an elbow resting through the open window, in a very debonair manner. He has seen the driver of a 14A double-decker do this, and thinks it looks very manly!

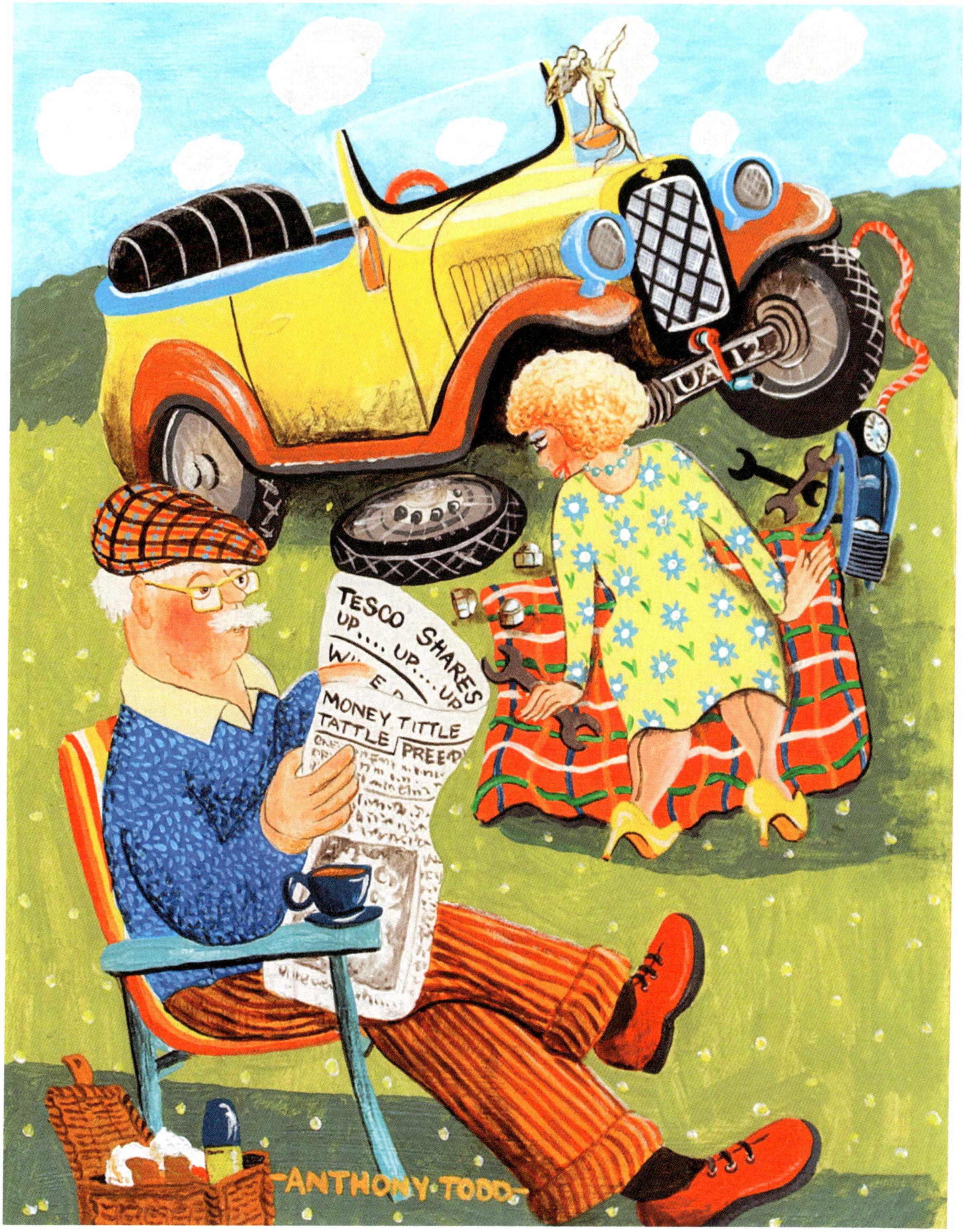
TESCO SHARES UP.... UP.... UP
MONEY TITTLE TATTLE
UA 12
ANTHONY TODD

The 'Borrowed' Scooter

Dotty holds on for dear life as Uncle Albert takes her for a country ride on his Vespa Scooter.

It really belongs to Micky Finn, the fish man. He delivers his wet fish on it, but today he has loaned it to Uncle Albert in exchange for a bottle of Dancing Dave's Turnip and Carrot Champagne.

To impress Dotty, Uncle Albert has polished the Vespa until it gleams, but he cannot get rid of the fishy smell, which seems to follow the scooter around. This proves to be Dotty's downfall. A few minutes of corner swerving and being thrown from side to side, plus the heavy aroma of stale haddock is just too much for her; Uncle Albert's new, hand-knitted jumper is ruined!

Dotty walks home with a headache.

Uncle Albert demands his bottle of Turnip and Carrot Champagne back.

Micky Finn tells him to 'bugger off'!

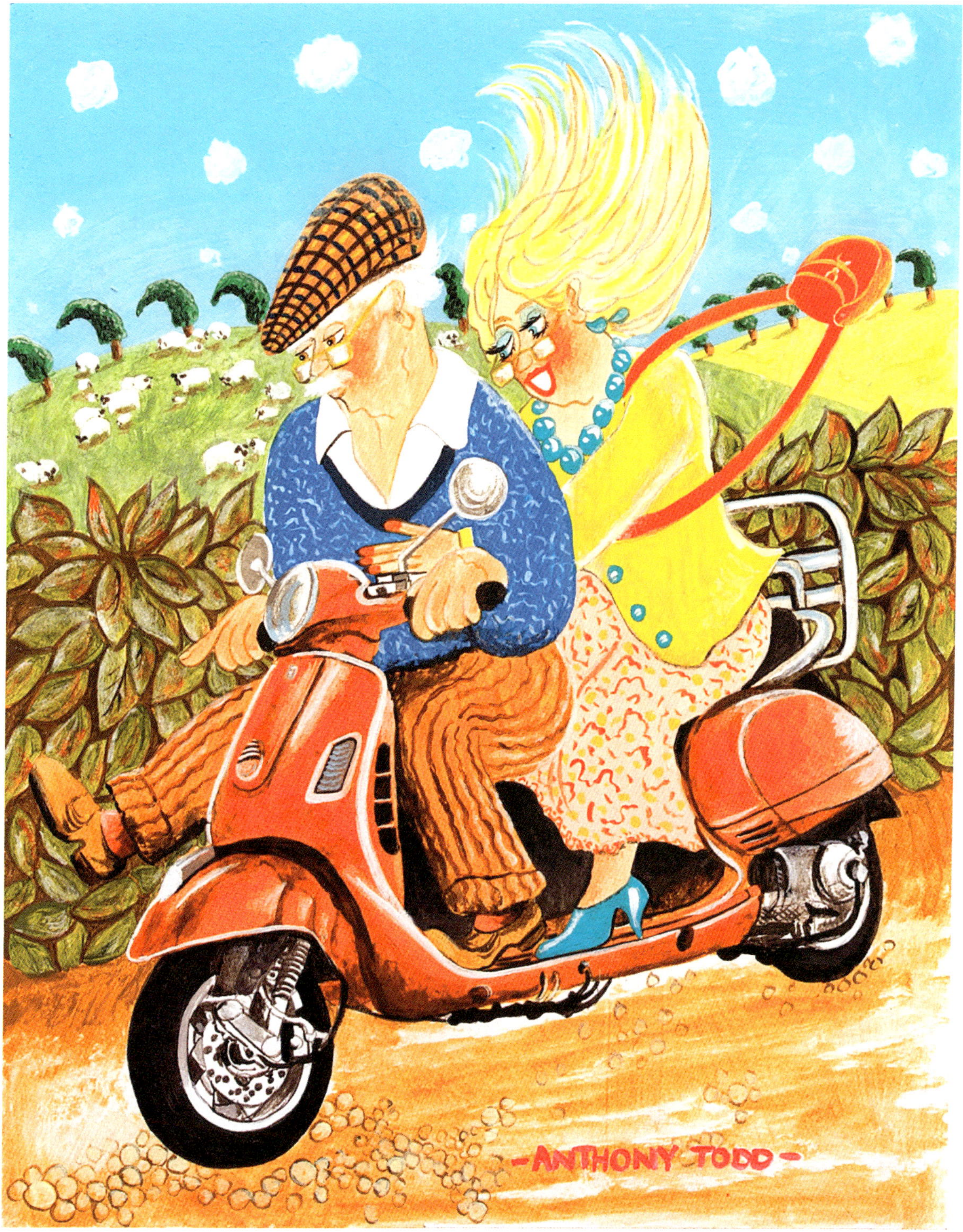
-ANTHONY TODD-

Flaming June

Flaming June has only won one race, and that was because the other pigeon developed a nasty cough in mid air and had to retire. Her name is really June, but race after race she would come in last; sometimes several hours after the others had finished.

Uncle Albert, who part owns her, with Micky Finn and Dog End Derek, would sometimes wait until the early hours for her to come home. They would shout out into the night all sorts of rude things to entice her in. "Where is that flaming June!", they would shout - and the name stuck.

Dotty thinks Dog End Derek can't wait for Flaming June to retire. He has said, more than once, that his Doris makes a lovely pigeon and bacon pie with thick gravy. Uncle Albert says he doesn't know what he is talking about, and besides he rather likes a nice rabbit stew with dumplings.

Dotty thinks they should all be ashamed of themselves and become vegetarians.

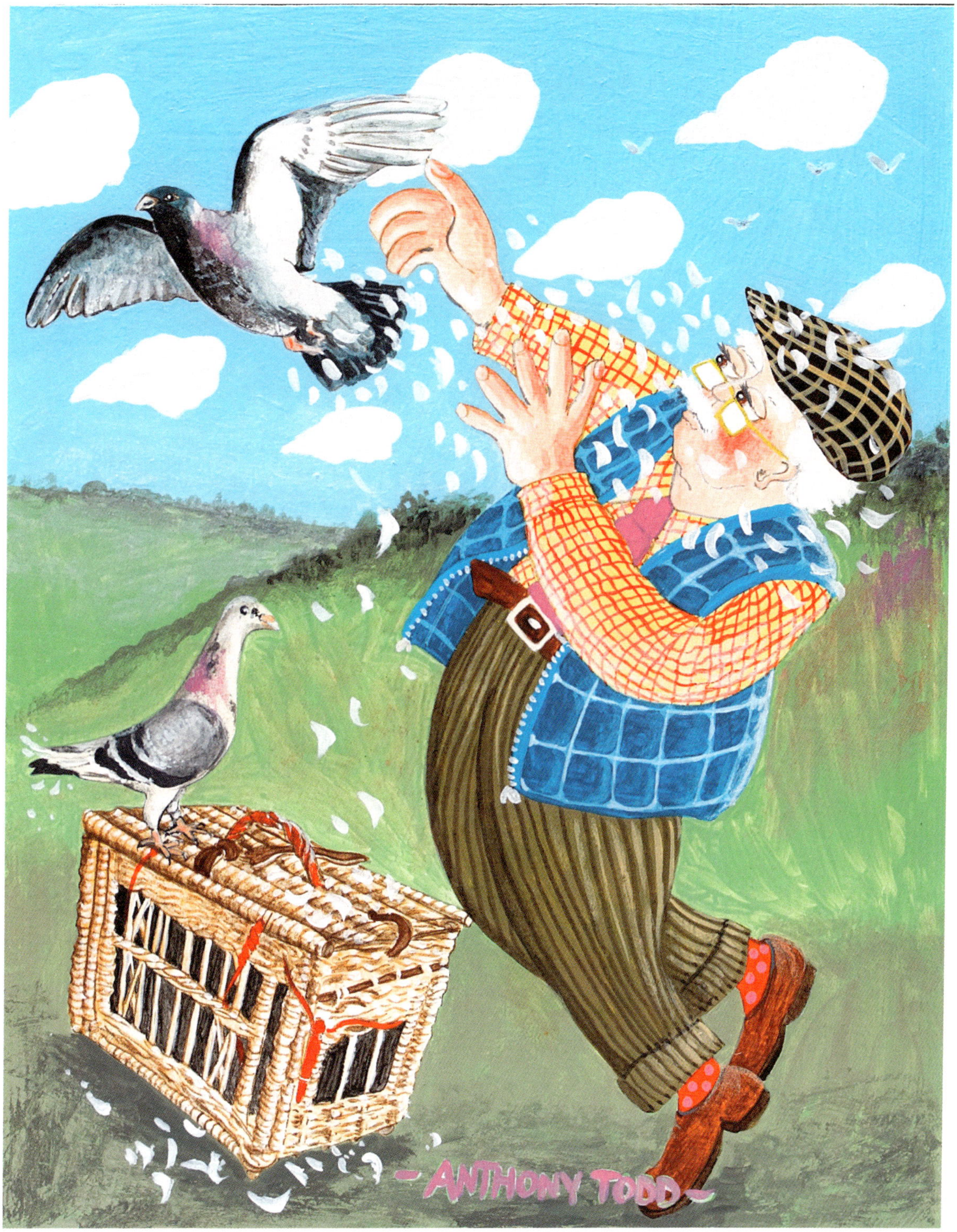
-ANTHONY TODD-

Did Anyone See the Blazing Firecrest?

When Rupert, from the Bird Spotting Club, said a rare Blazing Firecrest had been spotted, everyone rushed up to the common. They hid in the bushes, their cameras and binoculars at the ready.

Uncle Albert was determined to catch sight of this rare bird and had brought his late father's naval issue binoculars with him. These highly polished binoculars had never missed a thing, and if anyone was going to see the bird, he was. Monty could only see a sort of green mist through his telescope, and Old Jonnie Rotten was so excited by it all he clean forgot to use his binoculars and squinted feebly through the foliage. For an hour they hid without seeing a thing.

Brenda turned to Uncle Albert to say she was going home and shrieked "Don't move, don't move!" there, perched on Uncle Albert's head, was the elusive Blazing Firecrest, calmly preening itself, scattering feathers over his best cap. All, except for Uncle Albert, stared with wonder at this spectacle. Suddenly, with a puff of feathers, it was off. "Oh dear, you missed it Uncle Albert!" cried everyone in unison.

"**I don't care**", he mumbled, wiping feathers and droppings from his best cap, "I think it was a robin anyway."

The Lucky Rabbit

Dancing Dave fails a late fitness test for the Old Boys Kick About. His chronic wheezing has got worse, so Uncle Albert takes his place as a substitute goalkeeper.

They really want someone to score goals, but Uncle Albert's veins are playing up and he can't run very fast. In fact, he can't run at all, so they think he is best suited to be the goalkeeper. His war wound is also giving him gyp, something he never talks about, unless you're asking.

Amanda, Dotty and Brenda show their support and produce a lucky stuffed rabbit as a mascot. Uncle Albert thinks it a bit soppy, but hangs the rabbit up in the goal net for good luck.

As Uncle Albert attempts an exciting, arthritic dive, Spike, the dog, leaps into the net to see the rabbit off. Uncle Albert misses the ball, which bounces off Spike's head, and the rabbit is tipped over the bar by a confused goalkeeper.

Although losing seven-nil, Uncle Albert is declared hero of the match because of his spectacular save. Spike and the stuffed rabbit were never mentioned again.

Brenda thinks she has a cold. She lost her voice for a week, but Dotty says it's because she was screaming her head off at Uncle Albert. Amanda is now deaf in one ear.

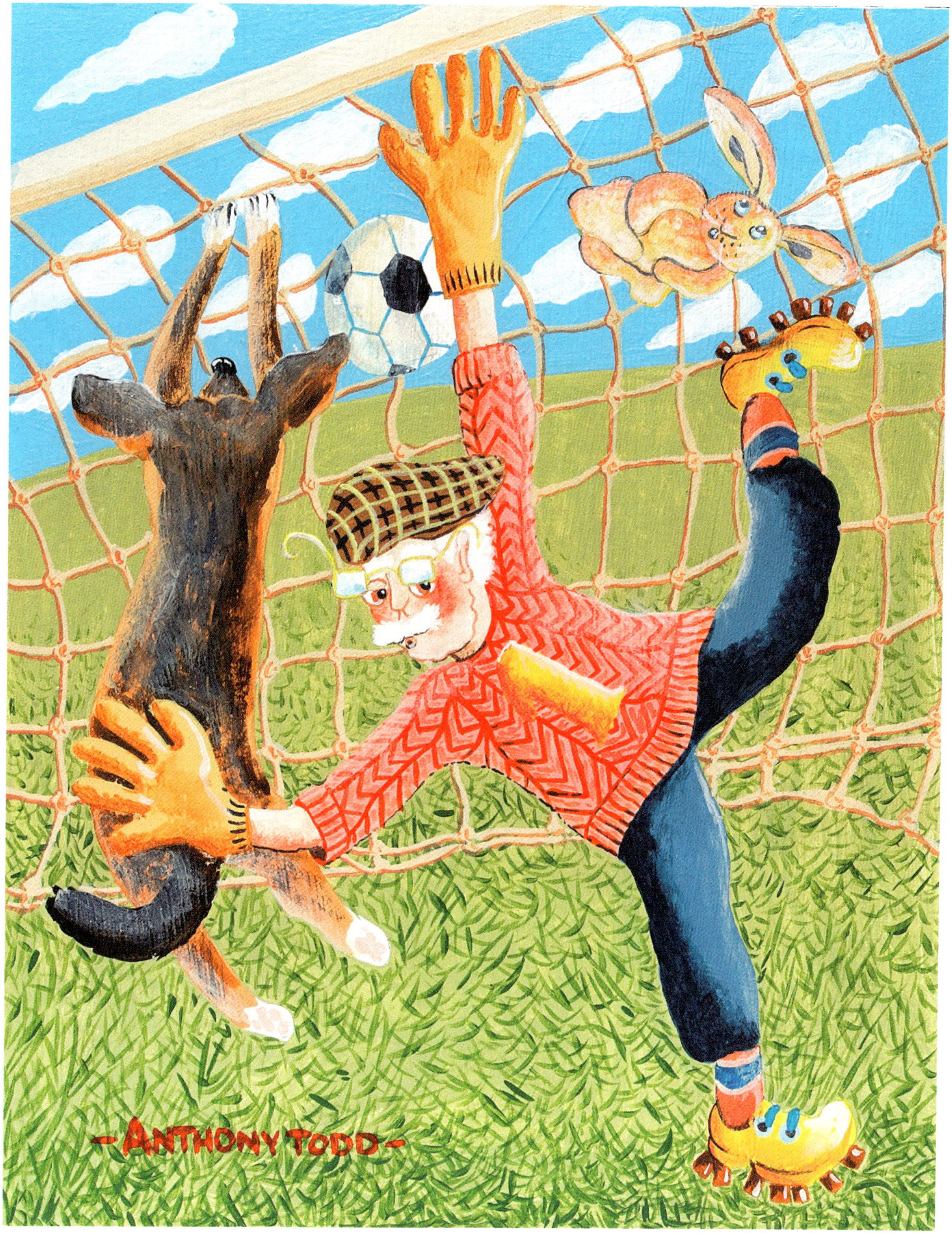
-ANTHONY TODD-

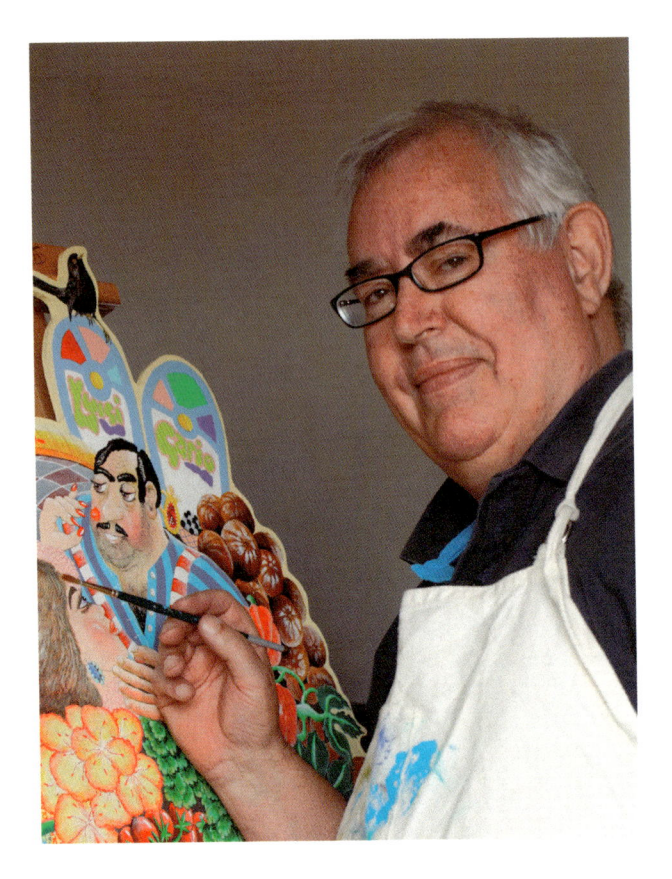

ANTHONY TODD was born in London and educated at Guildford, Harrow and St. Martin's Schools of Art. He paints and writes from his small studio situated in the Tillingbourne Valley, surrounded by the beautiful Surrey Hills. He has been married to Iris, a teacher, for twenty five years. They have two cats, Poppy and Daisy, who spend much of their time asleep in the studio. The cats love posing and appear in many of Anthony's paintings.

Made in the USA
Charleston, SC
08 October 2013